Po[illegible] Paradise

Carmen Willcox

Illustrated by
Lisa Elizabeth Berg

Published by CC Productions

Paradise Farm
Westhall, Halesworth
Suffolk IP19 8RH
Fax: 01502 575 886

ISBN 1 85525 035 7

Design by Red Hot Media, Lowestoft

Printed & Bound by Richardson Printing, Lowestoft

Introduction

The moment one gives close
attention to anything, even a blade
of grass, it becomes a mysterious,
awesome, indescribably
magnificent world in itself.

Henry Miller

This book's predecessor "At Home In Paradise" began as my personal jottings, simply notes to myself to enable me to record and recall events; sights and memories I did not wish to loose, much in the way I might have used a camera to capture moments, experiences.

In "Pocketful of Paradise", I continue this journey, noting how years may pass or things may change, but some reassuring core always remains the same. Leisurely or busying sounds, glimpses and glances of darting or wandering life. All Nature's tapestry constantly weaving and reforming itself into new and also into familiar patterns.

February

Wednesday 3 February

A very amusing sight kept me looking out of the bedroom window for a delightful minute or two earlier this day. It was a motionless Isis and Amber who were standing side by side by the pond's edge. In all their young lives, they had never seen a sight like this. They discovered what moorhens could really do best. Up until now they had only seen them either shuffling about in the leaf litter or plonked snugly in the green washing-up bowl. Now, here were the moorhens in all their splendid glory, gliding along the surface of the pond at top speed. From time to time they would do a graceful turn and produce beautiful ripples. The full range of their aquatic skills was on display for the two staring, humble, land-bound hens standing gob-smacked by the bulrushes. I felt quite sorry for Amber and Isis. They looked like two small children who could not join in with the party games.

I have not managed to catch sight again of any bluetit interest in the nesting box this month. Neither have I seen the woodpecker for quite some time now. I have not given him up, but still look frequently towards his favourite tree, to see if my patience is rewarded.

FRIDAY 5 FEBRUARY

Indoors the fire is kindled;
Beechwood is piled on the hearthstone;
Cold are the chattering oak-leaves;
And the ponds frost-bitten.

Sappho

One of the coldest days this year, and also the day when we had a leak in an outside water pipe. This meant that a very frozen plumber and I kept trotting about looking for stopcocks and drains and doing all the things that you just do not want to do on a freezing cold day. Each time I began to warm up indoors, I had to venture out again for some water and pipes-related reason!

The cold, grey day continued to thicken with fog. Late afternoon and Barry called me outside to show me the Barn Owl who was perching on a gate post by the long meadow. We watched this beautiful visitor till he flew up and disappeared among some trees. He always leaves a magical feeling behind him when he has graced our lives with his welcome presence.

SUNDAY 7 FEBRUARY

It has been incredibly warm today - unbelievable after the cold spell during the week. The fog has persisted and this

I really like. A misty day always makes me feel so good. In the late afternoon I felt in a creative mood and went across to my office to record a short story I had written last Saturday. It was a rather spooky one, so the misty greyness helped me with the atmospheric aspect!

I enjoy both listening to, and reading stories and poetry aloud. I am by far a greater fan of the radio than I am of the television. Somehow the senses employed when listening can be more enlivening and exciting than when too much is provided, as it is with visual entertainment. Also, for some reason, there is a greater feeling of intimacy and reality when listening to something being read or to a play being enacted.

Monday 8 February

It does seem as though Spring has sprung! All the wood pigeons have been cooing and our doves are pursuing one another amorously for much of the time. Added to all this activity, the doves are to be seen making frequent trips in and out of their little houses, carrying twigs and sticks in their beaks. They look brisk and have an air of serious intent about them.

* * *

Each day the chickens are heading off to bed noticeably later. It is a sight I always like to witness. First, old loner Jasmine heads off purposefully. She likes to be independent. The rest stay out to play longer. They fuss about and enjoy a last drink and croon and gradually begin to drift closer to their gate. Eventually, Apollo decides, quite suddenly, that it is time to retire.

So he makes the announcement and struts to lead the way ahead. He walks tall and proud, each step determined and strong, flanked and followed by his devoted wives and his teenage, still somewhat vacant son, Shogun. All the hens file in unresisting procession. They waddle away from the world and turn the corner to stride through and into their pen. Occasionally, one will have been left a little behind the rest and in her solitary panic, she races up, her fluffy, feathery bottom is the last thing we see, as she too, rounds the corner to disappear in with the rest - to enjoy a good, long sleep, squeezed up together with all her warm, soft, clucking, sleepy tribe.

Tuesday 9 February

My lovely mists continue. Not everyone's favourite season, but so undeniably soft and mesmerising. The memories of Avalon, Camelot and romantic, legendary days; these moments return to us from centuries long dead. They come back to us in these drifting images of vagueness and mysterious beauty. In their lost shadows, we can glimpse figures, swathed in veils, the cold shimmer of a sword, or the silent hooves of a galloping horse, vanishing amongst the trees. There is so much to see, on days like these ...

Saturday 13 February

The mists drift on. We move like ghosts; we mingle with the grey that is everywhere, and even the colourful pheasants and chickens disappear silently, enshrouded in wispy veils of invisibility. Everyone I meet with, speaks of feelings of overwhelming drowsiness and I well know it is this clouded embrace that is enchanting us all, as in the tale of the Sleeping Beauty. We succumb, we fall into the spell; the nebulous web of misty slumber.

Spin your elfin charms,
And from mad fingers
Let glad silks unwinde
Angelic webs
With silver'd souls entwined.

Kevin N. Roberts

Sunday 14 February

Saint Valentine's Day, and the first daffodils have opened - how timely. They are but a few, ensconced in a warm, sheltered corner, yet they made the effort to bloom for today's special day.

Wednesday 17 February

Despite the cold days we are having, our hens continue to lay well. They are not deterred as they leave the flock and head with bustling determination for their nesting place. They are wilful little creatures. Barry constructed the perfect nesting box. It corresponds exactly to the dimensions given by all the expert books on such advice. Yet still they persist in choosing their own spot. Nothing has induced them to move from their sacred nest. So much so, that if more than one hen at a time wants to lay her egg, she will get as close as possible to the already occupied nest, by lying on top of the first hen! It is true to say that their eccentricities are a great source of amusement to me. The more I get to know each individual character, the more interesting their lives become, in my eyes. I have often thought of devoting this whole journal to the story of their lives.

Saturday 20 February

For some long weeks there have been major works up by the railway crossing. From my attic window I could see in the distance numerous and often very bright lights as the work was carried out in the dark of late at night. Often even past midnight. If the wind blew in the right direction, I could even hear the very distant voices. Now at last, all is quiet, dark and back to normal. Strange how all that activity, though far from the house, somehow made itself felt. I suppose as one becomes accustomed to silence and not much happening, any slight disturbance becomes a focus of attention. Were this to take place in a busy town, it would scarcely be noted.

Sunday 21 February

The upper skies are palest blue
Mottled with pearl and fretted snow:
With tattered fleece of inky hue
Close overhead the stormclouds go.

R. Bridges

Generally, I consider February to be the least exciting month of all. Today however, Nature has literally strewn our lives with pearls. Amazing hail was fired in generous amounts and the scenery lay bejewelled all around. We later heard that several roads nearby were closed or diverted because of flooding. Suddenly, that feeling of February being the least dramatic, picturesque month has somehow changed.

THURSDAY 25 FEBRUARY

A splendid sight entertained us during breakfast - which was, therefore, pleasantly extended. In the old orchard, at the back of the house, a brilliantly coloured cock pheasant was trying hard to impress a timid, fleeting female. She played well the role of a coy, sensitive creature. Her soft, muted colours and large eyes gave her a subtle beauty. She escaped him, she turned away from all his attempts to captivate her. Pursued and pursuer were repeatedly interrupted by a strolling moorhen who felt it was her right to wander about in search of breakfast. She was constantly in their way and seemed unconcerned by their chase and courtship. Deliberate and unabashed, she persisted in her meanderings till at last the pheasant couple disappeared into the wilderness beyond. Finally, left in peace she calmly continued her morning stroll.

FRIDAY 26 FEBRUARY

As "broody" time draws near, it seems that Apollo is becoming more attentive to his hens. He tries harder to find them nice things to eat and when such food is found, he clucks dramatically, loudly encouraging, indeed insisting, that they come and feast on his offering.

His favourite wife is Opal, and he always makes a big fuss of her when she is near. It is Opal who is always most ardently greeted when she returns from having laid her warm, brown egg and it is Opal who sleeps beside him most often. The other day, after she had left the nest-box and called out her sing-song to Apollo to escort her back to the flock, a frantic Apollo raced to find the gate to their run was locked. He was nearly out of his mind. He pranced up and down and up again trying to get in to greet Opal, squawking all the while. He was the most upset I had ever seen him. His dignity thrown away in his screams and dashing about. What he didn't know was that the second gate was open, and when Opal found her way out of it and appeared behind him his joy was uncontained. He now clucked contentedly and immediately searched the ground for, and found her some dainty morsel to eat (probably an insect of some kind). He kept on with his attentive ministrations for some minutes till his anguish subsided and he felt at ease once more.

Yes, she really is the darling of his heart!

SATURDAY 27 FEBRUARY

The wind is blind,
Is blind alone. How he has hurled
His ignorant lash, his aimless dart,
His eyeless rush, upon the world,
Unseeing, to break his unknown heart!

Alice Meynell

The promised arctic weather finally arrives. Between the bright bursts of glittering sun we slowly but very surely become engulfed in impenetrable hail, utter darkness in the middle of the day and hard-driven snow to blanket our world. As it begins, Colin wraps up and braves it all to put out extra feed for the wildlife out there. No sooner is he indoors that from all corners of the garden they all come flocking to their various feeders and corners. The birds, the pheasants, the moorhens - All except the chickens who didn't make it to their pen and are taking shelter in the cosy, hollowed centre of a giant bush in the straggly, old orchard. All we see of them is a disappearing red crest, now and again. They stay there for a long time.

Indoors, the weather makes us lazy and we, too, slow down. There seems nothing better to do than to gaze in deep silence at the white world outside. We light a few candles and listen to the wind howling and whistling in its glorious power. It is good sometimes to just take time to look, listen and to just Be.

March

Monday 1 March

Trees are sanctuaries. Whoever knows how to speak to them, whoever knows how to listen to them, can learn truth.

Hermann Hesse

John Rogers and his bevy of lovely ladies arrived this morning to begin our long-planned, long-awaited tree planting. We have been in love with this project from the moment we first considered it, and now at last it has come. I feel very happy and excited. And in my mind's eye, can already see the grown trees as they will look one day!

Friday 5 March

Still the tree planting goes well, Neat work, artistic design and pleasant company into the bargain. At lunch time the "planters" come into the office and animated laughter travels from the back room where they "picnic". There is something different and appealing about people who work with Nature. A kind of clarity, an open joy. I suspect it is infectious too, fortunately.

* * *

Saturday 6 March

After a particularly busy week, I had been looking forward to an extra hour in bed this morning. This was not to be. I was wrenched into complete wakefulness by the unusual voices of two "stranger" cockerels outside the bedroom window. Strident and confident, they went on and on till I got up. I do not know where they came from or where they went, but obviously their sole purpose on earth was to keep me from sleep, this day. When they vanished, they left a small black hen behind. She was totally lost. All day she explored this and that corner. She dug, she clucked, she sunbathed. She made herself quite at home. She found all the conveniently placed watering holes and when we tried to move her away so she would find her way home more easily, she only did so for a while and returned to this, her new-found home. She is a lost little soul, black, tiny and wandering alone. At one point she found herself flanked by an unconcerned, feeding pheasant on the one side and our own fowl flock on the other. She panicked for a minute, then ran to hide somewhere. Our chickens stared with incredulity at this fleeting form, with all their staring profiles, petrified, gazing in her direction. Later, when somehow she met them across the terrace, a small scuffle ensued. Fortunately Colin broke up the confusion and the mysterious newcomer fled. Luckily, none of ours cared to give chase. If she refuses to leave here, it would be better if the flock adopted her swiftly. I know hens can be merciless to strange invaders, but I rely on Apollo's love of peace and order to diffuse any confrontation.

*　　*　　*

Later, at night, we opened the door for Jupiter. It was a worthwhile move, for the sight that met our eyes was unimaginably beautiful. The moonlit, silver-drenched garden was astonishing. The ghostly light of the moon glowing through the mist-draped air was one of surreal splendour, breathtaking and bewitching. It could not have been more moving or lovely. I will carry this image into my dreams tonight.

Over the roofs the honey-coloured moon,
With purple shadows on the silver grass,

And there is nothing more in this great world
Than thou and I, and the blue dome of dusk.

Sappho

Sunday 7 March

After a long absence, the woodpecker is back! In the early afternoon, his familiar figure darted to the same tree he always occupied and we were delighted to watch him settled there for quite some time. It is good to know he is still around, safe and sound.

Monday 8 March

Another good sign. The bluetit has also returned. During breakfast I saw him poised at the small, round hole of the nest-box. He was there, looking in, for quite a time. Then, apparently having checked everything was acceptable and satisfactory he flew up a couple of branches and I eventually lost track of him. After all, I did have to get on with breakfast.

* * *

After breakfast, another recognisable sound drew me to the window. It was the small, black, hen. She must have spent another night in the barn or thereabouts and had just emerged for her breakfast. Chuckling to herself, she made for the old stone trough in the middle of the terrace and began to drink at length. Then she resumed her scratching, digging and foraging. A solitary figure, in the early morning light. Alone with her thoughts, in this vast expanse of world. More vast than she can ever know.

Tuesday 9 March

The mantle of night has long since fallen. The distant train rattles along the tracks hypnotically. And memories of the day are all that is left in the void of the dark. It is cold again, and the bright sun has sparkled all day in this crystal clarity. Despite the lack of warmth, the light has encouraged the birds to sing sweetly. And the bluetit has been spending much of its time around the nesting box.

The black hen today was joined by her fine-looking mate. A handsome chap with the most fabulous plumes for a tail. They were long enough to trail on the ground. They were so, so black, that they shone peacock blue in the sharp sunlight. Dare I say he is quite a rival in beauty to our own Apollo and Shogun. I wonder if the handsome stranger has come to take her back home, or will he tomorrow, grace again our garden with his swaggering elegance?

Wednesday 10 March

Over the years, we have had a bat or two sharing our house, or to be more exact, Colin's study. His is probably the warmest room in the whole house, and maybe they like this. Although occasionally they are to be seen flying all round the place, it is always to his study that they retreat. Today he discovered their new hidey-hole. A chink so small up in the beams that it seems impossible anything could squeeze in there. We can only suppose that there is a wider gap beyond what we can see, where the bat can more comfortably move around or even disappear into the maze of floorboards and ceiling.

This evening Colin went into the room to be greeted by the bat landing on his head. It did not settle long, but took off for another circling of its adopted house and then off into its coin-slot of a home. Strange, how unperturbed and self-possessed this tiny bat can live quite happily in this man-made cave of ours.

Friday 12 March

As always, the finest of daffodils have splashed their gold, all around my office. Those along the drive always take longer. But my window and door are already adorned and bright - Merrily heralding the warmth that is to come.

Saturday 13 March

A splendid day. The sun is warm and the air is sweet. Colin and Maurice have been working hard. At the back of the house some serious digging is taking place. They are moving out a few old shrubs to another site. The final plan is to open out the view more into the old orchard. It should make quite a difference to see more space stretching out beyond. It seems not to concern the wildlife. They appear to carry on as usual, not minding this exposure. I am glad, as I had feared they might feel deprived of the natural shelter they had been used to.

The chickens too, seem happy. They welcome this activity, as worms and other creepy crawlies are disturbed and swiftly eaten.

Sunday 14 March

Warmer still - we had lunch outdoors. Jupiter stretched out beside me, soaked up the sun. Tommy stretched out beside Colin, also soaked it up, but he purred into the bargain.

Behind us, a big peacock butterfly was visiting a bunch of daffodils. Tommy watched her, but he was too comfortable to make a move. So he closed his eyes again and stretched out more, his belly upturned to the sun, and carried on snoozing.

After lunch, Colin went to Jen and Will's to help with the willow cutting. He returned (looking quite tanned) with a bunch for us to plant.

Monday 15 March

Before breakfast Colin had been out planting some of the willow. (He now looks a shade more tanned). The last three days have been perfect for such an activity. There still remain a few more willows to go in. I daresay by the end of the week he will have his full suntan all topped up and complete for the summer.

In pale new dress
The little willow trees
Give themselves to the caress
Of the breeze.

Mumei

Thursday 18 March

Oh it is good to be in this season. There is so much newness, so much happening. Each day uncovers a new surprise.

For some days now, the pink blossoms have blessed us with their young petals, scintillating in the sun, and delighting our winter-tired eyes. The same with the pale green shimmer of the tiny, shiny willow leaves that gladly herald long days ahead.

At the front of the house the collared doves, sleek and elegant, gather atop the cider press and complete the perfect Spring image of contentment and harmony.

Tuesday 23 March

On a day like today, when the damp earth and the warm-scented air mingle and invade our senses, comforting memories of my childhood return once more. Vague and dreamlike, but very real. I recall the long summer months I spent in the country. The place was called La Cava, and it was a riverside village, small and wonderful, to me, a city child. Now I close my eyes and once more I smell the watery scent of the river. I hear the wooden oars slapping the tensile surface of the water. I see the people, the grown-ups of my childhood, busying themselves and talking about what always seemed important matters. Some carry baskets of produce, others bundles of mysterious contents. And all the while Nature's sounds punctuate the scene; geese somewhere, turkeys too, maybe a goat or snorting horse, cicadas, frogs. Always frogs; ubiquitous and intriguing. Frogs fascinated me the most of all. They are wonderful things; capable of the utmost immobility and astonishing speed. Their leaps defied capture and practically endowed them with the quality of invisibility.

Thursday 25 March

During the winter, and the pranks played by the vigorous winds, one of our bird boxes must at some stage have fallen to the ground. Colin discovered it and picked it up, intending to fix it back to the tree. Out of curiosity, he peeped into the tiny aperture. He was most surprised to find a startled pair of beady eyes looking back at him! A little mouse had taken advantage of the fallen box, and opportunely built for itself a very snug nest. It was crammed full of thickly matted horse, dog hair and my tumble dryer fluff. I only wish I had been the lucky one to discover such an amusing and cosy little nest.

Sunday 28 March

> *I went to the woods because I wished to live deliberately, to front only the essential facts of life, and see if I could not learn what it had to teach, and not, when I came to die, discover that I had not lived.*
>
> Thoreau

A dazzlingly bright but bitterly, bitterly cold day. Nevertheless we braved it and in the afternoon went to Butley Woods to see the charming carpet of daffodils. It is a romantic place and the trees, some silent, some groaning, live their natural life in an almost ancient atmosphere. It was practically deserted and did not seem spoilt by man and his modernity. Everywhere nature had been allowed to be herself. No trimmed and precisely manicured lawns here! No geometric obsessions of neat lines and borders. There is nothing more relaxing and perfect than to roam in the natural beauty of softly moulded landscapes.

At the end of our walk we said we would return. Next time we plan to visit another place close by and surprisingly named: Carmen's Wood.

Wednesday 31 March

On waking today I knew I would feel at ease. It was the kind of morning when one's skin seems to fit really well and my body and mind felt very good and comfortable inside of it. The temperature was perfect enough to wear the lightest of clothing. There was no glare in the sky, but a soft and fresh drizzle sounded gently on the earth and a drowsy mist gathered as the day wore on. It was the sort of day that is made for snoozing. Alas, though, I had too many things I had to finish at the office and so could not allow myself the luxury of an escape into the irresistible arms of sleep.

Now at last, it is night, 11:45, and having waited so many hours, I can surrender to the welcome call of the Dream-Provider. I will close my eyes and straight away drift into that other world of sweetest charms.

Amid the winter's greyness
When I dream
Of happiness,
The blue of April's perfumed skies
Wrap me about
With loveliness!

Utsunomiya

April

Friday 2 April

What a contrast. A dazzling day. The hens announced loudly that they wanted to be let out. It was so gloriously Spring-like that it seemed a shame to keep them in longer than necessary, so I unhooked their door and they bolted out like children out of school. With a great deal of noise they scampered out into the world of dust-baths, wild flowers, water troughs, and shady bushes. They are very happy in the Spring. It is their favourite season. Not too hot to make them pant like summer can, at times. Even old Jasmine is laying eggs again, and looking pleased with herself.

I decide to give them a treat and open the birds' peanut bin. Amber knows the rattling sound of the lid and follows me into the Utility Room. She is so keen to get the peanuts that she comes close up to the edge and standing on tiptoe, begins to help herself voraciously from the bin itself, craning and arching her neck and burrowing into the peanuts; her beak and head immersed in all this edible treasure!

She is the fastest eater in the tribe and I have never seen her walk away from food, having eaten till satiated. She is always the one to eat up every last scrap, although strangely, she is the smallest one of all.

FRIDAY 9 APRIL

The feeling is more distant now and I should have tried to write in the dark last night. Yet the moment was too lovely to change. The doleful moon glowed like translucent parchment in the pewter sky. Her light was a mantle of coolness on my face and I was ensnared by her silent beauty. She exerted such emotions and imaginings, that graced by her touch it would have been so easy to write - Yet how could I willingly take myself even inches away from her web of light.

And in the morning now, her subtlety is but a dream, belonging to the world of spells and fairy queens. But I fancy, now and then, that a trace of her coolness remains on my cheeks. Her good night kiss as I fell asleep.

EASTER MONDAY 12 APRIL

Loveliest of trees, the cherry now
Is hung with bloom along the bough,
And stands about the woodland ride
Wearing white for Eastertide.

A. E. Housman

It has been a welcome, leisurely day. We brought our outdoor table from the shed and had lunch surrounded by the hopeful chickens. They always enjoy sharing our picnics, and the contest to eat the most and the fastest is always led and won by Amber. Tommy and Jupiter spread themselves at our feet and lazed about in the sun for the rest of the afternoon. The doves cooed and pattered about pecking at invisible edibles and lulled by their comforting sounds I read a book sleepily. Gradually a breeze stirred, bringing in its voice a sense of movement and activity. My reverie was ending and I closed the book and went indoors followed by Tommy and Jupiter who also must have felt a little ruffled by this change in the temperature. Indoors, we all settled down again and enjoyed the rest of the holiday in the stillness of the warm kitchen.

Wednesday 14 April

Two new baby doves are down from their nest. They nestle close together for warmth and comfort, and when one moves a little way, the other shuffles along too, as if they are connected by some unseen means. They emit high pitched sounds and regard one with a piercing intensity. Later in the day, one of them looked rather alone and quiet. I went close to see if he was all right. He glanced at me disinterestedly. I touched him slowly and gently, so as not to startle him. He did not move. Unsure if he was well or not, I began to stroke him to see if there was any kind of reaction. This time he became more alert and chirped loudly at me, he even began to shuffle about in his little dusty corner. Satisfied that he was energetic enough and capable of looking after himself, I tiptoed away. Checking him a few more times, and last thing at night, I can go to sleep well relieved that he is in good health and tomorrow will probably be even stronger and more grown-up.

* * *

In the evening Maurice popped in to mow the grass for the first time since last year! It seems it is the week for bringing things out of the shed, after the long winter months.

When Colin and Jupiter returned from their walk, he excitedly told me that he and Maurice had seen the first swallow of the year! This is always a favourite occasion with all of us swallow admirers; and tomorrow I will be looking out for this swallow and the rest of his tribe, who have travelled so far to come and be our guests once again. As I write this, I feel so overwhelmingly happy to know that his warm, little body is nestling safely in his old place in the donkey shed.

"Welcome back, beautiful visitor!"

Saturday 17 April

Flowers ... have a mysterious and subtle influence upon the feelings, not unlike some strains of music. They relax the tenseness of the mind. They dissolve its rigor.

Henry Ward Beecher

The Cherry blossom is now at its most lavish. Effulgent and profuse, the masses of frothy flowerets bow elegantly when they greet the breeze. It is a real beauty and one could be lulled to sleep by its milky white clouds of blooms that sway hypnotically in the gentlest of dances.

Nearer to the ground, the brightly coloured tulips are also delighting us each time we pass them by.

*   *   *

It is again mushroom-time. Colin brought in the first of the season, clean and fresh they rested in cool colours till it was time to take them from basket to cooking pot, where the alchemy took place and they were converted into a tasty dinner. No doubt, we will be having many more such meals, in the forthcoming weeks.

*   *   *

Maurice informs me that the moorhens have two nests. One along the ditch by the vegetable patch. The other in the main pond, among the reeds. This one already has eggs in it, whereas the other one has not any yet.

So it seems they will temporarily abandon their washing up bowl, under the flowering cherry tree, in favour of the pond and ditch, which are probably more secluded.

> *Wildflowers are perhaps the most enchanting*
> *of all for me. I love their delicacy,*
> *their disarming innocence, and their defiance*
> *of life itself.*
>
> Princess Grace of Monaco

Monday 19 April

Every growing thing now, every creature, has cast off winter thoughts. And everywhere the smell, the feel, the sound of Spring is alive. The trees now are all dressed up in their best frocks of pastel coloured lace and flounces. And in the meadows, even as late as 8 o'clock in the evening, baby lambs are to be seen playing hide and seek. Their mothers have long settled down for the night's sleep, while still they frolic, hiding and peeping behind old tree stumps and around the slumbering bodies of the older sheep.

In time, they too will tire and slump on the grass, to give in to the night and to sleep.

Friday 23 April

I am wide-eyed, open mouthed and my heart gives a thrilled jump inside me. For through the back door, I see the small black hen that visits us, and with her are, what look like four small balls of fluff moving around her. She has kept it quiet. Brooding in some sheltered corner, and though I rarely leave home, this time I have been away for just a couple of days - and this is what happens! What a home-coming surprise.

The chicks are tiny, tiny. They find it difficult to scramble over the stone borders in order to follow their, also small, mother. Their minute legs can barely be seen beneath all that gorgeous fluffy, puffy, feathery blackness.

Their proud mother calls them to the feeding spot and shows them the ropes. With them to care for, she has become less timid and comes the closest to the house that she has ever been.

She takes them to the small dish by the old tree stump. In this bowl, I keep ground-up, baked eggshells which our hens eat now and then. I had never seen the tiny black hen, however, so near to the house. Yet today she brings her little ones to share this delicacy. They join in with their particularly engaging kind of enthusiasm, and in their excitement they jump in and out of the small bowl, continually. They look like some kind of jumping beetle, hopping energetically all over the place.

At one point one baby chick scratches his head with such vigour, that the very momentum is too much, and he knocks himself over. But he is so low to the ground, maybe only an inch, that he comes to no harm and he's up straight away and running round and chirping with his siblings.

SATURDAY 24 APRIL

After a whole year of getting along pretty well, today marked a change in Apollo and Shogun's relationship. Perhaps it was something to do with the Spring that made Shogun decide to challenge his parent. With never before seen determination, I am sorry to say that Shogun began to attack Apollo who was understandably amazed. Before too long it was developing into a serious conflict and I felt I should intervene in this, Nature's way. Yet my intention was difficult to actualise. Two fully grown cockerels can move at a fast pace and no amount of hand-clapping, whistling, bucket-banging or shouting distracted them from their territorial intent.

Even when I threw a bowl of cold water at them, they did not flinch. Maurice joined me in the chase all over the garden and round the house. It was eventually Colin, who with his longer legs and arms managed to break apart the duel. I was exhausted and glad to resume calm around the place. During the incident, all the hens had, needless to say, been squawking at the tops of their very strident voices.

Colin, Maurice and I spent a few moments gathering our breath back and mulling over the strange ways of Nature's creatures.

Sunday 25 April

This, it seems, was not to be a quiet Sunday; at least not the beginning. We had got up reasonably early and in a nice leisurely way I had decided to do some writing before taking a bath. Colin had to go to Bungay for just about a half hour.

He had not been gone ten minutes, when I glanced through the window. To my dismay I saw Shogun begin the same challenging dance he had done yesterday. I sprang into action, knowing that without Maurice and Colin to help me, it was wise to try and stop the fight before it became too serious.

I flung off my slippers and dressing gown and in less than five seconds I had put on my wellies and coat and was pelting down the drive, racing after the battling birds. This time Jupiter was a great help. Having observed yesterday's goings on, he knew what I was trying to achieve and he was marvellous. Between attempting to deal with the cockerels, I was acutely aware of Jupiter's sensitive and obedient moves. In the midst of all the chaos, running and mayhem, I could not help mentally noting his remarkable behaviour. For a dog never trained in this kind of work, he was perfect. He followed my every cue. Advancing or stopping or following or whichever instruction I gave him. It was so incredible. When I finally managed to grab hold of Shogun and stop the brawl, I began to think how much I might enjoy being out on some fen, with my Jupiter to help me round up my (at present) imaginary sheep.

For winter's rains and ruins are over,
And all the season of snows and sins;
The days dividing lover and lover,
The night that loses, the night that wins;
And time remembered is grief forgotten,
And frosts are slain, and flowers begotten,
And in green underwood and cover
Blossom by blossom the spring begins.

Algernon Charles Swinburne

May

Saturday 1 May

I could not have asked for a more perfect day on which to have my Birthday. Not only is it at the beginning of the weekend, but also it is a Bank Holiday. So in addition to having the weekend, there is the extra Bank Holiday on Monday.

As for the day itself, it is perfect. Well, really it began yesterday, with friends arriving with gifts. I felt showered with the good fortune of their love. There was an emerald silk scarf. A star-shaped brooch. An exotic kimono-style tunic. A wooden, hand-painted life size cockerel, to mention but a few.

And then as the rays of the sun were slanting rosily through my window, and the day was beginning to cool down, I looked up to see a figure walking slowly up the drive. His arm was held out, as he carried something, resting on his hip. It was a most beautiful basket, and the figure was Will. I went out to greet him, Jupiter by my side. Will handed me the willow basket. It was the first, he told me, he had made this year. The size, shape and shades of willow that it was made of were all in total harmony. Each basket that he makes seems to be more lovely than the last. I could not have been more happy. This special gift rounded off my day splendidly.

* * *

Throughout the morning, the course of pleasing events continued. I had slept particularly well, dreaming of a Caribbean island. I woke up, after a gradual and gentle awakening by the jungle of birds outside. On looking out of the window I knew I was going to have a happy day. My favourite weather was waiting for me. Colin and even Maurice later commented on it. It was mildly warm, but the most intriguing mist was all around. Not a breath of wind stirred. All was still, save for the wings of birds, fanning the warm air. And to complete the amazing strangeness of it all, there was the deep growl of thunder, rolling in the background. The air was moist and felt balmy on the skin, and altogether, the atmosphere was quite, quite magical. I cannot describe the scents, the quiet, the sensation of the day. But it very much felt like moving lightly, inside a tranquil, muffled dream.

When we cannot find
contentment in ourselves,
it is useless to seek
it elsewhere.

Francois de la Rochefoucauld

Monday 3 May

I look outside - and note how swiftly the daffodils have transformed into light little bunches of scrumpled-up antique lace. Pale and delicate they rest languidly, their frail necks drooping, waiting for time or the wind to turn them to dust.

Indoors, I keep a few. Shy and dry reminders of their first days of lusty blossoming and fresh beauty. They will replace the older daffodils I have kept since last Spring. Two years, two generations, side by side. Touching, meeting and leaving. The older ones I will lay down on a quiet place, in the garden, so they can be gathered into the earth again. They will merge their very sleepy dreams, their long memories of so many moons gone by, merge them with their new life, as they meet the dampness of the soil once more. It will be a kind of rebirth for them. Maybe I will place them by the roots of the jasmine tree, so they can blend, to become a part of its fragrance.

Wednesday 5 May

We recently dug out some bushes that lay between the old orchard and the back of the house. I was a bit concerned that the wildlife about the place might feel less sheltered; too exposed to us humans. How wrong I was. Since the clearance of the bushes, more and more activity and variety has resulted.

In particular a magnificent cock pheasant and his three elegant wives that are present almost all day and evening.

Today, one of the female pheasants was enjoying a dust

bath in peace, on her own. She looked relaxed, without a worry in the world. From under the shade of some shrub, came Gypsy and her small family. She obviously fancied the dust bath for herself and her little ones. She did not challenge the female pheasant, she did not attack. She merely waddled up close and looked at the pheasant. After about fifteen seconds the pheasant must have felt less comfortable, being incomprehensibly stared at by this small, black, short-legged hen and her noisy brood. She reluctantly arose from her comfy dust bath and stumbled off into the thicket of the orchard. Mission accomplished, Gypsy settled herself into the vacated spot and began teaching her babies how to perform the dust bath ritual. They copied everything mother did and I could have watched them for hours.
Later in the day, I noticed the same dust bath spot was being enjoyed by an ecstatic rabbit who was wallowing in the earth. I had never known rabbits did this, and even now find it strange.

All in all, I keep today's memories with me in a special place in my heart. For just a few fleeting moments here and there, Nature made me feel as though I were living inside a legend, a fairy tale. In just a small patch of land, so much colour and beauty unfolding their stories. All within feet of one another. Moving, calling, eating, playing. Chickens, pheasants, rabbits, birds, cat and dog - all retaining their identities, yet allowing one another to simply be.

I think as they are given security, peace and the chance to be themselves, they all get along. There are no pressures, fears, competitions. They are shown gentleness and they get to know quietness and to understand rhythms of being. Even Gypsy, the wandering hen who chose to stay and bring up a family here, has grown confident and swiftly fitted in with the rest of the animals and with us.

The real voyage of discovery
consists not in seeking new
landscapes, but in
having new eyes.

Marcel Proust

Friday 7 May

The young trees in the orchard are beautiful right now. In full flowered splendour they captivate the sun's moods, the moon's light, the wind's embrace and our admiring glances. They will be stunning later on, but meanwhile we are feasted by the prettiest display of blossoms, we could wish for.

* * *

As late as 7.30 this evening, a blackbird was still hopping about, mouth stuffed full of straw. He must have been in a real hurry to be working so late in the day.

Monday 10 May

Along with the daffodils, the cherry blossoms have disappeared. And I am sad, but with this sadness comes another sensation. The feeling of welcome and renewed joy, as I sense something wonderful in the air. It is the scent of the fragrant white lily tree. The one the chickens like to sprawl under in the hot June through to August months. Its blessed beauty brings me memories of hot

Summer and panting, glossy black Jupiter and blissfully purring Tommy; all out in the blazing heat of the day. As I muse on this and almost hear the Summer sounds of the birds and insects, I have to stop writing and give myself to enjoying these thoughts in my own private daydream.

Wednesday 12 May

I heard the cuckoo today. A call that sounds close yet distant, balanced in the air between some branch and my ear; poised between silence and music, and later, in the afternoon, I heard a soft thud and a small, afraid fluttering in the office. Like yesterday, a swallow had flown in through the open door and was trying to understand the nature of glass! I went across to him and cupped my hands gently, folding his wings alongside his slender form. Jupiter was very good and though curious, did as I asked him, and did not attempt to make a grab at the tiny creature. Then, still holding the swallow, I walked towards the door, and softly kissing the small, feathery head, I opened my hands so it could fly off. He was a treasure. A living gem of glowing colours and exquisite symmetry. One could hardly find a more perfectly streamlined and beautiful bird!

Thursday 13 May

I think the moorhens must have been gossiping and rumours have spread around our little pond, for word has got around that a nice meal can be obtained near the house. "Those humans come out now and again, and then food appears". These tales must have made Mr. Duck curious, for I looked up from my desk and there, between the office and the house, was this duck doing a marvellous job of vacuuming all the remainder of any food up through his bill. He was totally absorbed in this task and he was most thorough. For about half an hour he waddled among the doves and other birds who did not seem to mind this newcomer at their banqueting table. It just makes me wonder - what new unexpected creature will we see next?

Saturday 15 May

Colin spotted a pair of turtle doves feeding among our own white doves. Their slim bodies singled them out from our own complacently plump residents. And although I had never seen a turtle dove before, I knew that these grey-brown visitors were something new to our garden. As happens with most animals that come to visit, I have a feeling that these will stay around long enough to hatch a brood and bring it up before they are all off, and go wintering in Africa.

Sunday 16 May

I was reading the local parish magazine, The Sheaf, and noted with pleasure that an eleven year old girl from the village is the youngest of four Halesworth Middle School pupils to achieve a gold award in the Annual United Kingdom Mathematical Challenge. Apparently, this is a competition designed to test fourteen year olds, and awards are given to the top 6% in the country. So our young eleven year old is a credit to our small community.

* * *

At last the moorhen's nest has yielded its fruit. Today, a proud mother swirled all over the pond with her little ones. To see more closely, we used binoculars. It was a delight seeing them so close and clear through the glasses.

It is a month of amazing activity. All flying creatures are in a flurry, looking for food all day long, it seems. Today, the new turtle dove pair came right up to the doorstep looking for more food. They are fearless and venture close with ease. Seeing them so near, their markings look even more beautiful than I thought they were yesterday. After a long while, they sprinted off and flew towards the old orchard, which is such a jungled tangle, that they must feel well hidden and at home.

> *How many daisies can you count on your lawn?*
> *When you can count twelve daisies,*
> *Spring has come.*
>
> Eleanor Farjeon

Tuesday 18 May

Mr. Duck continues to visit at feeding times, leisurely inspecting the ground to seek out his favourite seeds.

The turtle doves too, continue to attend the gathering of so many species. And they feel secure enough to sit sunning themselves on the feeding patch, when all the eating is done.

I am constantly amazed at how much thriving wildlife can be found in just this relatively small space. Perhaps if we had acres and acres we could run a full-time wildlife park!

The rest of the countryside looks perfectly marvellous just now with even a few poppies already out. The

landscape is brilliantly mottled with them, and among the luscious green grass, sparkle the glorious buttercups and sweet daisies. It is a feast for the eyes. I can drink it in for hours as I watch the changing moods of moving sunlight and deepening shadows. In all its aspects, at different hours of the day, it is such a satisfying joy - just being there with the humble flowers. Though the gentle-coloured wisteria still festoons the outside of the house, its fabulous fragrance is diminishing all too rapidly.

Wednesday 19 May

It was quite a thrilling moment, when I was asked to do the Fortune-Telling for the Village Fete which will take place in a few weeks' time. I was strongly tempted to go ahead and do this. After working out all of June's dates, I knew it would not be possible. Such a pity. I very reluctantly had to decline this very exciting and fun opportunity. Next year I could try to plan things so that I can be free for this time when all the village can come together for a very interesting day.

Friday 21 May

The cow parsley is out, the bumble bees are buzzing and a duck is ostentatiously parading up the centre of the Halesworth Thoroughfare! He does not seem perturbed by the shoppers and passers-by. He is the most confident looking duck I have ever seen. Distinguished and looking very smooth and neat, he waddles up and down, promenading with great dignity, and feathered beauty.

Sunday 23 May

8 o'clock in the morning and a blackbird is merrily splashing away in the stone trough outside. For more than a minute he dives, he dips, he flings water every which way. It is a real pleasure to watch his joyous splashings.

While I enjoy this cleansing celebration. I also notice a clear, summery sound. It is the cuckoo. He calls and goes on calling till I forget to listen and his voice is distanced as I now distinctly hear, very close, the lowing of cows. This is not usual and I imagine someone must have just acquired one or two nearby. All the rest of the morning I hear cows; and I find it a soothing, restful sound. It is reassuring and tranquil, as if evening and sleep time cannot be too far away.

Monday 24 May

Today I hold before me two of the most intricately and perfectly designed treasures of Nature's marvels. They are light, strong, silky, furry, warm, cool, elegant, magical and stunning in their subtle colouration. They are two feathers.

On Saturday, a magnificent owl came to die at Paradise. To hold this majestic bird was a privilege. To stroke his wise head, touch his beak, claws and beautifully made feet was a truly impressive experience. The owl has a presence like no other bird. He does, indeed, seem to be the right winged one to accompany the ancient enchantress and the wizards of Alchemy. He appears to be more a part of man, a thinker, an intelligence; somewhat akin to how we see dolphins. Only this winged creature is a swimmer among the vastness of our spacious skies. I hold his feathers, and I mourn his loss. It takes a death such as the death of this beautiful owl to bring close to me, the reality of love, life and death and to know how interwoven they all are. To feel how they are all, almost one and the same emotion. How the boundaries melt away and we are left floating in a sea of pure sensing. A sea where we all merge and become one with the Great Spirit.

Our guardian spirits meet at prayer and play.
Beyond pain, joy, and hope, and long suspense,
Above the summits of our souls, far hence,
An angel meets an angel on the way.

Alice Meynell

Thursday 27 May

All night long it has rained most heavily. Thunder and lightning played their part too. This morning, great puddles had formed, they were more like lakes. So wide and deep were they that they even fooled a pair of ducks who were contentedly swimming about in the tiled yard. Soon all the doves were joining in and even the blackbird who nests in the fig tree, took to splashing also. He is a very opportunist blackbird and has found just the right spot to bring up his family. He has all facilities laid on: swimming pool, ready meals diner and lots of shelter to keep his family warm. When the hens are feeding, he flutters down, selects a variety of appetising morsels and flies home with full beak again - Home being just a few yards away. So he doesn't need to expend much time or energy either. Cunning bird!

Friday 28 May

After so many weeks of tender loving care, Gypsy has lived up to her name and gone a-wandering. She dismissed the four chicks and all motherly duties and skipped away in search of more exciting action. Later in the day, she returned. She had in tow a magnificently coloured and lavishly feathered cockerel with a high, sprouting flowing tail. His plumes waved in the breeze and glittered in the sun. Gypsy was obviously besotted by this handsome escort, and made all manner of ingratiating, crooning sounds.

She brought him to show me. They stood outside my office. She looked at me through the window and called for food. Obviously wanting to impress this feathered

Adonis, she was persistent in her request, until I went to the door and threw a handful of grain. Soon they had eaten it all and her escort turned away to leave. Gypsy was distressed by this sudden departure and she chased after him, clucking wildly. I think he must have been overwhelmed by this overt display of passion, because he quickened his pace. I lost sight of them in the wild-growing greenery. A little black hen with short, short legs, racing after her dream lover.

Meanwhile, her sad offspring mooch about nervously. They stick together and seem afraid of almost everything in this big, wide world.

I try and look out for them, feeding them whenever I can. Making sure they are not intimidated by our own tribe of hens. As late as 8.30, when our chickens had just gone to bed. The baby-four were still up and looking at the house pathetically. I knew they looked hungry and again I went out to feed one last time before bedtime. They cheeped and ran about among the food with a mixture of glee and desperation.

About half an hour later I thought I should see if they had found a secure place in which to sleep. I went round, peeping under every bush and into each nook and cranny and finally found them huddling close together, in a tight squeeze, up against the wall of Jupiter's room. I thought I would make it more safe and snug for them so I pulled away some weeds and nettles and closed the door; jamming it just enough to enable them, and nothing else, to be able to slip in and out when morning came.

Sunday 30 May

By the time I went outside, the four black chicks were already skipping about. So they must have spent their first motherless night, quite well, by themselves in Jupiter's old quarters.

The morning is a lovely one, bright and warm. There is a strong wind which shakes the trees and scatters petals, but it is quite warm and pleasant. Tommy has been sleeping in the sun and now he strolls in dozily, hawthorn petals resting on his head and flowing down his warm neck and back. He looks like he has been to a Fairy Wedding and got himself covered with magic confetti. He has no idea how pretty he looks, as I stroke him under his snowy white chin and kiss the tips of his owl-like ears.

Monday 31 May

Ah, rapture! My favourite roses are in bloom. Once again I can lose myself in their splendoured aroma, breathe in their glorious fragrance. There are just three blooms open at the moment, but many more buds are waiting to burst radiantly into this warm world. If nothing else is to be written about, today, then this is all I need to be more than happy.

It was the time of roses,
We plucked them as we passed.

Thomas Hood

June

Thursday 3 June

Each day some new surprise, some fresh colour dawns, in order to surprise us, and today it is the clematis outside my office window. It is a much admired beauty and each year it receives compliments from those who come to the office. We have recently moved the old elm bench from the back of the house to rest under this clematis. It makes a nice surround for anyone wishing to sit awhile and feel enfolded by flowers of gold and by the sunshine.

Monday 7 June

It seems the May rains have dispelled to leave us with warm days that burst upon us with sunshine. Everything, every flower, each blade of grass is so brilliant, soaked in the luminous rays that touch them all day long and in the presence of such glory we can know some of the genius that touched the great painters. We know that it is the light, the colours, the energy created by all of Nature that has given to us the gift of Art, of painters who by harnessing such beauty, bestow on canvas images which inspire us to treasure and imitate them. Artists expand our own dreams by plucking visions from the air and in their own style they paint, they give, they open doors so that life itself is intensified and can be absorbed over and over.

Each time I look at works by Rossetti, Blake, Moreau, Matisse... I cannot but feel a renewal of my own creative energies. They are a miracle, an inspiration. They extend to us restorative powers which can transform us and our world. It is not insignificant, that throughout the centuries, despite famines, plagues and poverty there has always been consistent support for Art. There has always been patronage from the Church or the Aristocracy to ensure that, at all costs, Art should continue; and in its way Art repays us down the ages by bathing us in its exquisite diversity and blessing our spirits with its healing beauty and, if you look at your favourite painting today, you cannot doubt the intensity of this truth.

THURSDAY 10 JUNE

How could I have known all those weeks ago, when Gypsy was just a timid visitor, that she would become the most faithful hen in the place! She keeps us regularly supplied with her daily gift - a small and beautifully shaped egg. While our own hens are getting into their old habit of roaming afar and not bothering to return to their usual nest. Now and then they have a good day, but on the whole, they have become rather careless.

Gypsy has now remained a permanent resident and sleeps

in a little patch under the kitchen window. She goes to bed quite early and I like to pop my head out of the window and see her black feathers nestled well under the foliage; ready for the night.

Saturday 12 June

Roses, roses everywhere! The front of the house is covered in masses of them. And the jasmine tree... How could I have missed its first flowering? Today it already has whole clusters of precious white flowers scenting the wind. As I touch the cool petals I find it difficult to believe that twelve months have gone by since I was writing a similar entry in my journal. But in the case of the jasmine, time cannot pass by quickly enough, as I am always so very eager to welcome back this most gracious of blossoms.

Tuesday 15 June

Almost Mid-Summer and everywhere the scent of Summer intrigues our senses. Now it is the honeysuckle which entices us. Sweet and soothing as the comforting smell of warm, rising dough. And even the humble little flowers that spring up in unexpected places have a distinctive charm, in this vibrant month of June.

I admire their vitality as I take a short-cut through the Churchyard. It is a lovely day and apart from the birds singing nothing disturbs the peace. Only a couple of elderly ladies enjoying a chat, sitting on a bench; lend a small background of sound that is soft and pleasant. I walk on and a robin flies up to a cranny in the Church wall. He has a wriggling worm in his beak and he looks at me fearlessly. We are only about three feet apart and I walk away slowly so I can get to gaze into his lovely eyes a while longer. But I cannot stay in his little, busy world, so I leave him and the Churchyard and move on to my next destination.

Sunday 20 June

I awoke with the strange and vivid memory of a dream. I dreamt that I was most upset by Jupiter having caught a beautiful young pheasant. In the dream I was angry at Jupiter and when I awoke I was so relieved to find that he was indeed innocent and he had committed no such act.

Later in the afternoon, I was just on my way out when something made me look sharply to my right. I was astonished to see Tommy hurrying towards the house, a baby pheasant squeaking in his mouth. To my astonishment, Tommy put the baby pheasant down as he came towards me. I do not know the precise reason why he did this, he is usually very possessive on the rare occasion when he catches a bird. Who knows, perhaps seeing me and Jupiter together disconcerted him. Whatever the reason, I was glad. Stooping to pick up the little waif, I was deeply relieved to see he was alive and very healthy. I tucked him under my blouse, to keep him dark and warm and went to find Colin to consult him what to do with my find.

We had two options, try and guess which of the various pheasant mothers he belonged to. The second was to chance slipping him under Gypsy's feathered body. Fortunately, she began going broody again, just a few days ago. And now, in her little nest under our kitchen window, she has a new baby already. We will see in the morning if any maternal bond has been forged. At least, when Colin slipped the chick under her wing she did not protest, as the baby pheasant snuggled under her warmth. If she adopts him though, this might mean the end for her two eggs, plus the three I added to see if I can assist Nature in the breeding of another Amber and Jasmine. Well, time will tell. And tomorrow morning will give us the first instalment.

Monday 21 June

Summer Solstice. And to its ancient honour I must have dreamt these very precious moments:

The feeling in the dream was second to none, the immense satisfaction, and deep fulfilment was overwhelming.

The dream is very special, for it is of a place which I have on a few occasions before visited in my dreams. It is an extremely powerful and sacred site. In the past I have always climbed up there alone, and seen no-one. It has always been a little fraught with danger, but the prize was so worthwhile.

This time I decided to take Colin there with me, as I wanted him to know the power of the place. We were long in arriving and, although it seemed many years apart, I did remember the terrain well. The anticipation whilst climbing was magnificent, and also knowing that after the viewing of the prehistoric Dolmens, and being among, in and under the tombs, that the climb down would be just as exhilarating. The descent was quite,

quite breathtaking. Not in actual landscape beauty, but because the energy contained within that winding path was so absolutely electrifying.

However, this time the dream was sadly different. On arriving there I sensed that others had also been there, and so metal barriers, like giant staples, made the scene somewhat ugly. The power of the Cromlechs was still strong, but man's intervention with his metal and his presence, was ugly. Nevertheless we got as close as we could.

Then I had an idea I approached one of the guards who was very young and would be less experienced with visitors. So I chatted to him for a while, and got to know him. He mentioned he remembered me from last time. "Remember, I am Spanish too" he said. I laughed and nodded "Ah, yes". "Tell me" I continued "Is there some chance we could get close to the Cromlechs when no-one is likely to know?" He was friendly, and so I was hopeful that we might manage to revere the sacred cell-like stones later in the day, when everyone else had gone.

Then this young guard went on to tell me how much he loved the stones too, and when he could be alone, usually on Saturdays when it was quiet, he would go into the main Cromlech (which was indeed my favourite stone circle too) and enjoy just being there in his meditation.

I remembered the inside of the place well, and knew exactly what he must have felt. Remembering, made me long for this tiny cell once more, and so I wanted to visit the stone cell again with its small stone shelf carved out of the rock itself, and its one or two simple stone bits of furniture, and chalice, and seat that had been kept in there through the centuries. Down, down through prehistory, it felt as though these Dolmens had been built by the very Gods that made the Earth.

Then I began thinking again of the wonderful climb down. The very, path of departure. All the hidden bends and rocks, and marvellous places of brilliant energy that were hidden from mankind, and my very soul swelled with Divine Light!"

It seems that here is an appropriate place to end today's entry. For it is not only in the first step we take, or in the middle of a life, or in what precise moment we control that we find meaning; but sometimes meaning finds us. For me, it always seems that an end is a beginning. As in the dream, where the prospect of the departure was so exhilarating, so maybe I will take this dream as a sign and, though unplanned, that the end is to be looked for and looked towards. Though this metaphoric end is here, tomorrow will begin yet another day, another new life, another mystery.

What lies behind us and
what lies before us are tiny
matters compared to what
lies within us.

Ralph Waldo Emerson

Saturday 26 June

All around the house, new little lives are warming under their feathered shelters. Gypsy, under the kitchen window still sits serene and entranced, moving only every twenty-four hours or so to bathe, preen, groom, drink, eat and celebrate her brief release. At the back of the house, a blackbird too, is sitting on her nest, with admirable dedication. Maurice found the faithful bird when he was clearing away some runaway shoots and creepers. She nests only three feet from the ground and appears most confident and relaxed. Having uncovered her hiding place, before he discovered her, Maurice placed back some branches. Now she is well hidden again.

SUNDAY 27 JUNE

For days now I have followed the unfolding of a sweet romance. Today I spent some ten minutes watching the heart-warming, soft clucking, tender togetherness of Amber and the unlikely Franco, our roving gypsy cockerel. He is devoted to Amber and follows her everywhere. When he is around, she croons softly and chuckles and nestles and seems to go all gooey and lovey dovey. Together, they sit for hours while the rest of the tribe scampers about in the sun. As I write this, I feel the urge to go out and catch up with the latest development in their relationship. I have a feeling she may go broody quite soon. I will keep you updated.

MONDAY 28 JUNE

A nice story to tell today. Though it is unrelated to Paradise. Clearing up some papers, I found an old fax which our Penzance shop had sent us some months ago. I kept it because I liked its contents so much. Now here it is for you to enjoy:-

A customer just came up to us and said "Do you know

you've got a pigeon sleeping in one of your baskets?" We laughed thinking it to be a joke - but there was!! It was having a groom, sitting all fluffed up and comfy (it's raining outside). We think it walked in! Wendy picked it up and we released it. It didn't seem to be concerned, it was very healthy and tame...

Somehow it is the kind of story which we cannot really believe, but it is so good to know that it is true.

July

Wednesday 7 July

Another story worth telling is today's. For a while now, one particular blackbird has been getting very regular with her visits to glean tiny remains from the chicken's food. Today she actually braved everything and transcending any fears in her tiny, birdlike heart hopped right into the utility room. As if this heroic feat were not enough, both the cat and the dog too, were in the utility room at the same time! Astonished, I gave her some raisins and we all watched her in absolute amazement.

Thursday 8 July

Well ... our intrepid blackbird has boldly broken the limits - she has sauntered into the kitchen to ask for her delicacies. No doubt she had been waiting outside long enough and decided to prompt us into action. After all ... she has a new brood to feed!

Tuesday 27 July

It is ages since Gypsy began brooding her eggs. Well over four weeks. I do not think anything is going to hatch. Meanwhile, Nature's little mishaps have lost her all but one egg. I do hope she will not be disappointed when nothing comes of her diligent sitting. Also, when she finally emerges, she will find her besotted Franco has disappeared. In her absence he began to get restless and challenged Apollo repeatedly. The situation got nasty, so we took Franco back to where he came from. He has not returned. It is a different world without him. I do miss his reedy cockadoodledoo. But now at last peace reigns, as Apollo placidly leads his tribe again.

Wednesday 28 July

The end of the month is close. Apart from a few sweltering days, this Summer has been a fickle one. Some days have felt decidedly Autumnal, yet occasionally, the air breathes a gentle warmth and then our senses are confused once more.

August

Monday 2 August

We were speaking with a neighbour who had been trying to scare off the birds from his crops. He apologised and hoped the sound of his gun, which he let off to alarm the sparrows, had not disturbed us in the early morning. He then went on to say that he wouldn't mind "borrowing" our sparrow-hawk. He was referring to the one I had seen on our roof some days earlier. Apparently he lives at Paradise, because according to Roy, he always sees it heading off home, towards our stables. It seems I am not as observant as I thought I was, as my own sightings of this lovely predator have been so rare.

Sunday 8 August

The evenings now tell us that Summer is tiring, retiring. The dark comes earlier, and I begin to light candles as dusk falls. A new quiet seems to enfold the house, as though the day's rejoicing celebrants were in an eternal slumber. Try hard as I might, I can hear not a thing stir outside my window. It gives a certain curious feeling of being all alone in the Universe. It is dark, dark black tonight. And the world could be worlds away! So deep, almost religious is this soundlessness, that I would like to continue working all night. Being singularly, totally alone in this my silent, desert island, I receive insight and energy from the tranquillity which softly surrounds me. It is at times like this that I feel truly and blissfully at peace. At times like this, the music of Silence bathes me in heavenly purity.

In quietness are all things
answered, and is every
problem quietly resolved.

A Course In Miracles

Tuesday 10 August

Beautiful moments at this time of year. Blackbirds bring their young to the house. They show them that here they can get all manner of food. Their favourite being the sun-soaked, rich tasting, fruity raisins that we offer them. It is essential for Nature to get off to a good, healthy start, and mother blackbird seems to agree with us that raisins are just the ticket.

The baby's shrill, insistent cries encourage the parent to feed it. It is amusing to see the baby spit out the raisin. The mother returns the rejected fruit to her offspring's beak. Once more it is flung away. The performance is repeated three or four, sometimes five times. Eventually, the baby gives in and takes and eats the raisin. It is all a very entertaining episode and I feel a little lost and sad when they fly away and the scene before me is left empty and silent.

MONDAY 16 AUGUST

The young apple trees have begun to yield their first and lovely fruits. Fresh and shiny they taste full of summer and bird song.

Each bite gives up its share of sun energy, till now stored inside the smooth, fragrant skin.

Later in the day, I find two magnificent, healthy looking snails. Barry was clearing away some overgrown corner of the garden, and these two shelled creatures, their home disturbed, began moving. I held them for a long while, snails being one of my favourite animals. Later I had to reluctantly let them go. I found them a quiet and damp spot, well away from where the chickens or birds would find them. I know they will now remain undisturbed and well.

WEDNESDAY 18 AUGUST

This Summer the weather has been playing hide and seek with us, but today the sun is out. The crystals which hang from our windows catch the bright rays and transform them into rainbows. These rainbows cast their colours around the room, on walls, floors - and today - on a spider web. It is a remarkable effect; the delicate strands painted oh so softly in a multitude of hues.

FRIDAY 20 AUGUST

Curiously, the sparrow hawk has been quite active these last few days. Today a pair were circling above the poplars. They were very vocal, screeching and making their presence very noticeable. I can only guess at a couple of reasons, but have no way of really knowing.

Later in the afternoon, Barry was clearing out some excess weed from one of the ponds and called me over when some newts were resting in the net. It is always a pleasure to look at these little swimmers close up. And seeing them today, certainly brightened up my outlook. I walked away all the better for knowing they are still living close to us.

Saturday 21 August

Shortly after waking up, I went to the side door to see if any of the doves or chicken visitors were waiting for breakfast. Some mornings they are earlier or later, some mornings they want second helpings! This morning I was to get the most perfect gift. Gypsy was on the doorstep, and close by her feet was a fluffy ball of golden yellow. At last she had hatched one of the eggs we had substituted. After almost two months of sitting and some failed and broken eggs later - we decided to surreptitiously introduce some of Amber's and Karma's into her nest. I don't know who is happier - Gypsy or I! I was really taken aback for some seconds. The world disappeared, and all I could focus on was this little beauty and its chirping voice. Instantly I named her Angel. The name suited her as she had a golden halo-shape on the top of her head, and also she is born this weekend of the Angels Feast (U.S.A.).

Presently Colin returned from his walk with Jupiter and his eyes nearly popped out of his head - It is a miracle, each time a new fluffy appears in our lives.

Monday 23 August

The poppies behind the house look festive and bright - This new site seems to suit them well. It is the first time we have had poppies here and each time we glimpse them, they are a welcome surprise.

Friday 27 August

It is very entertaining to see the golden Angel interacting against her black bantam mother. Today, Angel became engrossed in her foraging. She found herself following the wrong hen by mistake. She had been assiduously pecking here and there when she pulled up in mid stride. She peered at the pair of legs right in front of her. Then up to see, not Gypsy her mother, but Amber! She turned and ran off squeaking loudly till she was reunited with her mother.

It is not only the young chicks that supply endless stories to watch unfold. The other day, Gypsy and Angel were consuming the special delicacy we had saved for them: cheese.

From a little distance. Franco had been watching and thought he might like to try some cheese himself. He approached them, stole a piece and made off with it. A few feet away he started pecking at it. Gypsy would not tolerate this behaviour. She strode up to him, picked up the well-travelled piece of cheese in her beak and took it back to Angel. Franco dared not repeat his daring move again.

September

Monday 6 September

The agile bantam mother does not know her chick (offspring from a Rhode Island Red egg) cannot fly up as high or as easily as a bantam chick would. She effortlessly flies up into the giant flower pot, outside the shed. Angel, in an attempt to emulate her, flutters her wings like a humming bird, and is rewarded by just making it up there. Once she has joined Gypsy, she teeters a little, at this great height, before settling on the rim of the flower pot. Some moments later, she lets out a high-pitched chirp and dives into the soft earth inside the pot. Together they both croon, and burrow, and dust-bathe, flinging soil particles merrily and noisily.

* * *

Angel is now old enough to eat raisins whole by herself. Previously, she or her mother, would batter them on the ground to make them into little-beak-size pieces. She is well on the way to being independent and less vulnerable than a couple of weeks ago.

WEDNESDAY 8 SEPTEMBER

Five o'clock, and the light of day is less intense. The day is ending, and Tommy encourages me to unwind. He invites me to join in his world, and together we play under the willow tree. I have found a dry branch with withered willow leaves. It makes a nice, rustling sound. It is ideal for chasing, make-believe it is something else. So I gently brush his paws with its tips. He dilates his pupils. He stalks. He twitches his tail. He pounces on the trailing branch. We repeat the game over and over. He pounces, and rolls and leaps high into the air. All the while we are intent on our game; working together, so engrossed in our complete involvement that time has no meaning. Time and all else, have disappeared.

Wednesday 22 September

"I am not this body.
I am Me.
I am the Spirit God created,
Free!"

Apollo died today. He had been steadily declining in health after an injury, during a duel with Franco. There was nothing else we could do for him, to give him back his health. We were bruised and heartbroken. We allowed him to go to sleep with dignity. He has been a magnificent example of powerful strength and gentleness. We shall miss him always, I do know that.

Thursday 23 September

Tonight, under the Equinox Moon, we gave Apollo a burial of the love and respect due to him. We placed notes and tokens of our love for him, in his grave. Now he will rest from his pain and join his family, that journeyed before him.

* * *

Just as Death comes to take our loved ones, so Life gives new joys. For the first time, today, Angel displayed great vitality and skill. She flew right over the astonished Franco's head. Chirping and flapping her golden wings, she glided over him, landing some way beyond him to join her mother and aunt Isis. Angel was clearly pleased with her new-found talent, and for a while continued strutting and preening and exercising her little wings. I am grateful to this Angel, for in her beauty and grace, she is helping to ease the ache of Apollo's absence.

Monday 27 September

For some weeks now, the pheasants have begun their secluded calling. Invisible but loud calls, like rusty hinges on rusty gates. But today they have been boldly parading and strolling about the place once more. Their welcome presence is always a delight. Their colours and exotic elegance never fail to arrest my attention and admiration. Thank you for returning to us this Autumn.

Tuesday 28 September

Our Parish magazine, The Sheaf, carries a nice article this month. It seems our village has won the "Village of the Year" competition. Though these days I find less opportunity to join in on the events, I am still happy that this award has rested on our small community.

October

Sunday 2 October

The poppies at the back of the house, have all but gone. The last trace of summer fades fast. It has rained every day since last Saturday, except for today and a little respite on Thursday. We must start feeding the wild birds, soon. That really will be the first sign of wintry days to come.

What the west wind whispers
At the end of summer,
When the barley harvest
Ripens to the sickle,
Who can tell?

Sappho

Thursday 14 October

Today is really and truly the chilliest day of the season. My bathroom was 52° even by 9 a.m. so this decided me that the heating had to go on if we were to be relieved of this North wind coldness.

Sunday 24 October

Outside my office window, the valiant poppies still stand. Radiant amidst clouds of green and yellow and white. Not a time for flowers, yet these small, resilient beauties stay on to greet my mornings and give me joy.

*   *   *

It is dark today - The clocks have given us a new perspective on our evenings. The spider above the kitchen sink doesn't know this, however, as she lets herself down on her thread. She does this in order to sip at some water drop, for her night cap.

Friday 29 October

This is one of the saddest days. The feeling began when the lovely Angel did not skip to our door, demanding breakfast. Her chirpy voice will never sound again. Her neat, small head will never again turn to look at me, as I bend down to hand-feed her.

Her absence spoke loudly. We did not want to hear what it might say. But we had to listen and look. We looked in all possible places and in all unlikely places. There was no sign of Angel.

At last, Colin walked down the drive and out of the gate. It must have been painful to find Angel there, flung into a ditch by the crushing blow of a speeding car. The sight of her would have devastated me. Imagining it, was enough.

Her fluffy, white, softest feathers were left behind, on the road. Too beautiful to be soiled, yet now soiled and bloodied.

My days will be much emptier now. My mornings much less cheerful without her young voice and flirting little wings to win me over and bring me to greet another new day.

"Thank you Angel, for all the sweetness you have given me during your short life."

December

TUESDAY 23 DECEMBER

It has been too long since my last entry in this Diary. What prompted me today, to write, was the welcome surprise on my desk. I noticed my violet was putting out the most bold little buds! So sure of themselves and full of determination, they were prettily showing themselves to me from beneath the dark, sheltering leaves. They thrilled and amazed me. So early and unexpected. I had been looking forward, as I do every year, to welcoming the profusion of violet flowers that brightens my desk, my whole day. Frequent are the times when I have been deeply absorbed in admiration, drinking in the riot of effulgent purple, darkest green and vibrant yellow that are the colours I know so well. Tenderly I care for and smile at this small friend who watches over everything I write. We exchange glances and thoughts. And when I water and feed her, I marvel at how long we have been together. Many seasons, years of companionship. Some people have come and gone, yet she still remains, healthy and contented as I turn her, from time to time, so that all sides of her take turns in watching the world, the other side of the window. She sees all kinds of weather and faces all the moods of the sun. We enjoy our silent communion. Brown eyes, Violet petals. Both relating to each other in our different but wonderful language.

Wednesday 24 December

Christmas Eve and the butterflies seem to have decided to have a party. Coming down to breakfast, I found one sitting on the table exactly where I place my plate or bowl. Later and throughout the day and evening, more butterflies emerged from nowhere. They were flying around the dining and sitting rooms. Eventually, I had to capture some and put them in another room, so they could cavort to their hearts' content. My concern being that they are so tame and come so close, that it would be too easy to inadvertently damage one. They seem to like settling nearby, on a cushion, on a book, on the dog's back. Wherever there is warmth or activity, they seem to like joining in. I am much more relaxed when I know I have housed them in a less visited room. Deprived of our presence, they entertain themselves by perching on windows or resting on the carpet. Strange, beautiful little creatures.

Tuesday 30 December

A wide-eyed female pheasant flew up onto the sitting room window sill this afternoon. She seemed dazed at her own audacity. Generally shy creatures, this was quite a daring step to take. We looked at each other in mutual surprise. She remained for some minutes, savouring her chance to survey the interior of a human dwelling. When she finally flew away it was with calm and poise. I felt really proud of her mature conduct.

*   *   *

Finally, the first violet flower is fully open. My smile said "Well done, and welcome to another Spring." Now that the blossoming has begun, I feel a kind of encouragement in my own daily activities. It is some reminder towards movement. An empathy. A mirroring of intentions which helps to direct and to motivate. A companionable collusion that seems to say:- "Right. Now I've made the effort to start flowering, so you get on with your own task too." And with such a glowing example I cannot fail but get on with things and do my best to move on with the day and all that it brings.

> *We must learn to look on plants not as mere points of colour, but as old friends on whose coming we can rely, and who, returning with the recurring seasons, bring back with them pleasant memories of past years.*
>
> Henry Bright

January

WEDNESDAY 14 JANUARY

The year has begun with a backward glance to the past. Reminiscences of a distant time, even before my birth.

This evening we visited Rita and Albert, "from across the meadow." Inevitably, as we toasted all manner of good wishes for the new year, we began recalling much of the past. Albert came here in 1928 and so has lived here for well over half a century. He has much to tell. For instance, he told us that what is now our small pond, once used to belong to his land. And much of Westhall collected its water for their own domestic use. It is strange to think of our little pond, being such a focal point of village life, at one time. We also laughed at how differently we both regard our gardens - while he cares for his immaculately, with shrubs and neat pathways, we tend to keep, or rather, allow ours to "express itself" more freely. He is a dedicated gardener and Rita is marvellous at growing the most sumptuous and exotic blooms. Her conservatory is a perfect haven. It has a truly peaceful atmosphere. I almost wish I had a small writing desk there.

Often, as I sit at home and write, my thoughts go back to something Albert told me some years ago. It was a sad and romantic story. It took place about the time of my own birth, when someone whom he described as a very "attractive, classy lady", bought Paradise Farm. According to Albert, she did a lot of work on the house and brought out all the old oak beams. Her husband was an artist and sculptor and she was going to fix the barn so it could become his studio. Alas, their dream was shattered, as he died just before they were to move in. Though, apparently, she stayed in the house for about four or five years.

I often wonder, had he lived on, what marvels he might have produced, inspired as he no doubt would have been in this lovely and magical place.

Wednesday 21 January

Today, I met with a friend. Inevitably, at some point during our conversation, we alighted upon the weather. Somehow, this led to the stormy gales of October 1987, which was a very memorable time for me, because it was that precise week that we had moved to Suffolk. I had lived in Yorkshire during the '70's and early '80's and I thought that had prepared me for any and all manner of blustery and formidable whims of Nature. Yet here I was, barely unpacked in my new home, being utterly astonished at the raging winds and spectacular energies that were being unleashed. After a sleepless, incredibly noisy night, I made my way out to the garden and fully experienced the roaring and buffeting and gusting of heaven's wild breath. Reminiscing with my friend, I told her how I had wandered outdoors for a while, until I found two broken branches on the ground. I had matched two, almost identical, "L" shaped ones for a very special purpose that was going to make my life easier. My friend was listening, mystified. I unfolded the story: Upon moving into Paradise Farm, we had very little furniture, and one thing the bathroom lacked and really needed was a towel rail. Upon the wall, two deep holes had been mysteriously left, though at a very convenient height. So, with my two magical, little branches and some wood glue I ran upstairs and promptly created a wonderfully rustic, perfectly fitting towel holder, in the form of the two newly gathered sticks - which I now hooked into the wall. And to this day, well over a decade later, they still serve me faithfully and more prettily and nostalgically than anything I could have bought! Rounding off my story, I saw my friend's eyes wide with amazement, as she had followed my recounting of this, very dear to my heart, little tale. Then we both burst into laughter at this really quite odd idea, that such a momentous, historic date should be partly enshrined in a bathroom as a modest towel holder.

If you wish to know the divine,
feel the wind on your face
and the warm sun on your hand.

Jack Kornfield

February

Thursday 5 February

A very pretty morning. Spring-like, bright and filled with bird song. Nice too, that I felt in quite good spirits. Then, on my way to the office, I was even more uplifted... rounding a corner, I chanced upon Isis. Something was moving around her feet. I quickly realised, with a great leap of joy, that it was her newly-hatched brood of two gorgeously fluffy chicks - One black and one, palest gold.

Oh, such a glorious moment. To hear her clucking proudly and her little ones calling with loud chirpings and much wing-fluttering, in order to keep up with her long strides.

I think we shall call the pale chick, Jasmine, to remind us of that venerable, old girl, who died last winter - she was the oldest hen we have ever had the pleasure to know. As for the black chick, I am not yet sure, maybe something nocturnal, like Shadow or Midnight or Stella. We shall see...

Tuesday 10 February

Both babies are progressing well. Though, the other day, Stella fell into one of the water bowls (the only one we had forgotten to place a stepping-stone in for their safety) and luckily I saw her struggles to swim out. By the time Freddie and I had run outdoors, she had fortunately managed to clamber towards the rim, and so, on to safety. But it could easily have been a less happy outcome. Immediately afterwards, Freddie sank into the bowl, two sturdy stones. So we can now be more certain that such an accident will not be repeated.

Monday 16 February

Some things in life do seem to foresee the edicts of Fate. This morning, on my way to the office, I noticed Isis had only baby Jasmine with her. Stella was nowhere to be found. And no trace at all of her disappearance to give a clue as to what had happened. Sad and strange, how having known her little chirpy form for only a few days, I could already miss her so much. Fortunately for Isis, I don't think her arithmetic is very good and so she seems, luckily, unconcerned. Though it would have been nice for Jasmine to have a tiny companion to grow up with. I only hope that Isis does not give up her mothering too soon, as she did with her first chicks. They used to follow her all over, not understanding why she was being indifferent. She, on the other hand, had other plans. She began incubating a new batch of eggs as soon as she was able to.

Monday 23 February

All through the winter, beneath forgetful white, these tiny entities remain asleep, recharging their energy until the first thaw of spring. Then, as if touched by magic, within days the mountainsides bloom with patchworks of colour. The miracle of nature once more unfolds.

Princess Grace of Monaco

Crocuses and snowdrops have once more been heralding warmer days. Though some days still turn out chilly and frosty. The brighter daylight is making us all active and very intent on a spree of reorganising and rearranging, both at home and in the office. Stacks of accumulated papers and boxes and odds and ends are being cleared out, making us industrious and giving us more space. It is a joy to find ourselves freed from clutter and able to breathe, more clearly and deeply. Once this whirlwind of tidying begins, it becomes difficult knowing where and when to stop, as we go from room to room, seeking to transform all that we come into contact with. It is comical to see everyone, in his or her own little corner of the place, trundling bundles and bags and boxes filled with goodness knows what defunct remains of useless bits and pieces. Very soon, all of Nature too, will begin its own flurry of activity. In their case, this shall be the opposite, taking the form of collecting materials with which to build and furnish their nurseries.

Friday 27th February

When I was a child, and lived in Spain, my mother was fond of "making ponds." Whenever we were out, walking in the countryside, she would wait till I was distracted. Having absorbed myself in some world of my own, I would forget her presence. It was then she set to work. She would find some fragment of discarded, broken glass. Then proceed to clear a small space in the earth, by scraping away pebbles, weeds, and so on, to expose the darker soil beneath. The shard of glass would be placed exactly right, so the sun would make it sparkle. Then she arranged tiny stones, sticks and flowers, all around its edges, thus concealing its true nature.

After this was done, she would call me excitedly and pretend she had just found a diminutive pond. This miniature miracle looked, to my young eyes, just like the real thing. And I would be amazed and awed. At the same time, I sort of recognised it for what it really was, but my febrile imagination always won out, convincing me it was a magical lake. The haunt of mystical creatures, fairies and other unknown, tiny beings. To this day, I can envisage the beauty of this enchanting, captivating world of mysteries. To this day, I can bring to life the sense of wide-eyed discovery, and smile at the excitement that these magical ponds created in my long Summer days.

Today, as we arrange for our real, life-size ponds to be cleared and refilled, my mind returns to those far-off days of innocent wonder and wide-eyed acceptance of all that was new and charming and possible.

March

Thursday 12 March

For many days now much watery activity has entered our daily routine. Gerald and Ian have become part of the landscape as they laboured from early morning to late evening, through drizzle and chill wind, to bring fresh life to the ponds.

First, they carefully transferred the water of one pond, into the other pond nearby. Then, all the many years of accumulated sludge was skilfully and painstakingly removed. When the clean, healthy layer of clay was reached, the water was returned, freshly filtered and fresh water too. Now all the ponds' inhabitants have a better chance of survival. This huge task has opened up more possibilities for the vitality and proliferation of any watery guests that find their way into our little ponds.

The chickens also, have found this to be a favourably eventful time. The tractor churned up deep tracks in the meadow and like a flock of hungry seagulls, all the chickens dived in the soil, left in the tractor's wake. All manner of edibles must have surfaced, but not for long, as quick beaks darted here and there, with amazing eagerness and speed.

Tuesday 17 March

Pharaoh and Treacle. A more devoted couple, one rarely sees. Early each morning, the impressive black and iridescent feathered Pharaoh jumps up to the top of the hen house gate and swoops down and into freedom. Closely followed by his besotted Treacle. True to the name, she sticks close by him all the day long. Wherever Pharaoh struts, Treacle runs to keep up with him. Never letting him out of her sight, as she battles her way through the tall daffodils, on her short, little, fast legs. Often, he will scratch the ground and dig up some delicacy for his clucking love.

With much excitement, he calls to her and presents his find. Then proudly he stands back and watches her appreciative enjoyment as she eats all with great relish. On and on, throughout the hours, they wander in happiness together.

When, in the late morning, we let out the rest of the tribe, Pharaoh and Treacle still remain enamoured of each other, seldom separating or straying too far with the others.

Wednesday 25 March

I am a nocturnal person. Reaching my most alert peak as evening falls. So my mornings are more like vague dreams, rather like an unconscious "getting about". Often, I feel as though I am watching someone else moving around, instead of it being really me. So when this morning I became aware (but only dimly) of something dark and furry on the kitchen floor, I had to force myself to wake up fully and begin a nursing campaign. The tiny blob on the floor was a very weak and distressed bumble bee. She really did have very little life left in her. I quickly set about to get a small sheet of paper from my note pad and went to get the jar of honey. Then I dripped a generous droplet of honey in the middle of the paper and lowered this on the floor. Gently, I eased Mr or Ms Bumble Bee onto the paper. There was no strength in the tiny legs or wings and barely any movement at all so I had to carefully slide the exhausted creature towards the honey drop. The very same instant that its head neared the honey, the long proboscis darted out and began to feed at this golden nectar. I watched as the honey began to disappear as its restorative power was transferred to a now very happy Bumble Bee. One hour later I went back to find all the honey eaten and an energetic buzzing at the window told me the treatment was completed.

I opened the window and out flew a renewed life, with one very full tummy.

Sunday 29 March

In the woods, I feel that
nothing can befall me in life
- no disgrace, no calamity
which nature cannot repair.

Ralph Waldo Emerson

Thankfully, today has been a simple, peaceful day. The hours passed and it seemed a day well spent, punctuated by two pleasant rediscoveries. Strange how something already known can bestow renewed pleasure.

The first of these occurred whilst I was out, strolling in the meadow. From afar, I glimpsed a tiny cluster of yellow, then another and another. On arriving at the spot, I was happy to confirm my surmising. The little tufts of yellow were the first cowslips of this year. Warm and friendly as ever, they clustered and peeked up at me and made me glad. Their familiar shapes were somehow reassuring. As if they exuded a confidence in their growing. A kind of optimism that signalled the way towards the nearing months of long and bright hours and more flowers yet to come.

My second nice surprise was in chancing across the almost forgotten tiny gravestone that someone, many years ago, must have placed in the garden. This is dated 1783 and bears the initials MM. Its mystery will never be released. But it is engaging to think about its origins and history. And each time I meet this enigmatic relic, I find myself gently slowing down and coming to peace and somehow detaching myself from any thoughts or cares I had been carrying.

April

Friday 3 April

More and more flowers are daily making their appearance. Colin has planted hundreds of bulbs and, everywhere, a riot of flouncing colour is invading the garden and surprising forgotten corners and adorning the grass all about the roots of trees and in between mossy stones.

Seeing all this variety of blossoming beauty is much like hearing the many instruments that flow together to compose a spirit-lifting symphony.

Saturday 4 April

Jupiter and I went outdoors to watch the rain. Sheltering by the kennel, Pharaoh and Treacle were standing close together. Feathers touching, merging colours. In a corner, nearby, Dodie stood alone. Presently, he began his distinctive chirruping song. Whether this was to cheer himself up, or to attract Treacle, of course I shall never know. But certainly, the sound of his charismatic song intrigued Treacle. The sound is soft and warm and throaty, and almost without any breaks. It must be as fascinating to hens as it is to me, because when he "sings", I always stop to listen and on this occasion, as if spellbound, Treacle began to walk round Jupiter's kennel, following Dodie's voice and joining him in his solitary corner.

She moved close. Right up to Dodie, leaving her, usually beloved Pharaoh, behind. And there, by Dodie's side she remained, while Pharaoh suddenly became aware of her absence. He began looking for her, not realising she was on the other side of the kennel. He clucked and called for her, but she did not join him. Then he found two pieces of overlooked bread and kept up his call, to offer her his new-found meal. Eventually, he decided to eat the two pieces of bread himself, comforting his disappointment. He headed towards the hen house, but remained under the willow, staring at the rain, perplexed, no doubt as to her whereabouts.

I do not know the outcome of this story, as Jupiter and I decided we'd seen enough rain for one day, and we both went back indoors.

And you feathered flute-players,
Who instructed you to fill
All the blossomy orchards now
With melodious desire?

Sappho

Friday 10 April

I awoke early. It was 5.20 a.m. and the world outside was eager and bright. Hunger propelled me to the kitchen, where I enjoyed a fresh snack of celery hearts and cottage cheese with pineapple. Watched by Tommy, who enjoys my surprise forays into the refrigerator, I shared with him my cottage cheese and upon finishing, I went up to my attic. It seemed too early to really get up (since I had gone to bed at just past 3 o'clock) and yet I felt too awake to go back to bed. Once in my attic, I drew back the curtain, opened the window, and was immediately greeted by the most astounding sounds of bird songs. The air was wonderfully fresh and balmy and misty. The birds, what seemed multitudes of them, were unusually vocal. The whole effect was stunning. I leaned out into the mist and was wrapped in layer upon layer of exquisite singing, warbling, cooing, trilling. Mesmerised, I took my portable cassette recorder, switched it to "Record" and balanced it perilously on the outside of the window to capture the doves, the pheasants, the hundreds of birds and hopefully the breath of the mist, too. After some time, I headed back to bed. Later in the day, when I arose, I retrieved and played my amateur recording. Although not of excellent quality, of course, it was nevertheless, magical.

Saturday 11 April

Today, a friend of ours, arrived to visit us from the States. His flight had been over thirty hours and though exhausting and challenging, he soon felt restored upon breathing real air. He was, unquestionably tired, but merely the sight of the bustling chickens, and the softness of the grass under his feet, gave him a burst of joyous energy. He was overawed by the way Nature restored him to calm. And for our part, it felt so good to see anew, through his eyes, all the simple beauty around us.

Monday 13 April

Our American friend, today, received his first lesson in the duality of Nature. Alongside all the many wonders and gifts we enjoy, there has to be the occasional sad loss or disappointment. Today was one of those upsetting times I so dread. We found, dead, a magnificent Tawny owl. This is always one of my most harrowing moments. It is with no exaggeration to write that I truly feel such a painful despondency. It stays with me for days. The image lingers. A perfectly created owl. Majestic. Noble. Beautiful. Dead. The feelings of deep sadness always mingle with a thankfulness and pride in the fact that he chose to come to rest in the safety of his final home. There were no visible signs of the manner of his death, so Fred took him to a Lowestoft bird specialist to have an autopsy done in order to, hopefully, find out the cause of death. We often do this, with the rarer birds, as it is, I think, important to find out if there should be some particular reason or common denominator.

Tuesday 21 April

How ironic. How appropriate and how beautiful that even as death brushes our lives, new life is always present. Our young, small white hen is sitting on a massive egg hoard. So big, she cannot cover all of it. We could not understand this, as Colin had left her with just enough eggs to sit on comfortably. But today, Fred discovered the culprit of the growing egg mountain. It was Isis! Apparently, Isis has been laying her own eggs in Snowy's nest, a staggering total of thirty-seven were crammed in, under the mother to be. Fred said she found poor Snowy pushed up into the corner, while Isis insisted on adding today's new egg to the already huge collection. Hens can be so stubborn when egg-laying, diligently adhering to their habits. It will soon be time for the new eggs to hatch. We shall see the results...

Tuesday 28 April

Once more Nature tricks and surprises us. One never knows what will greet our morning. This time it was in the shape of a seemingly dead chick, half in and half out of his shell. But, before you are saddened, there is a happy ending. Upon picking up the cold, half shelled egg, Freddie assumed all was lost. But we have learned never to give up, until all has been tried. So Colin placed this half-alive, half-hatched chick close to the Aga.

When I went to see it, it was a strange sight indeed, a long leg sticking out of a tightly packed shell. After some time, I did not think the chick had enough strength left to complete his emergence. He was tiring. He was quiet. I tried to encourage it by gently rocking the egg in the palm of my hand, and by making mother-hen-clucking sounds to which it responded in high pitched chirpings. But the shell was too strong and though I gently chipped and cracked it a little, it was obviously still not enough for him to escape from. So with great patience, lots of time, some drops of warm water and continued communications, I, in turns, moistened, cracked and peeled away tiny fragments of shell being particularly careful around his face and eyes. By mid afternoon the birth was complete and a lovely black and white chick was alive. I decided to call him or her, April. The energy he remanifested now, was quite amazing. And by nightfall, we transferred April, from his Aga nursery to under his mother's wing, who welcomed him with such gorgeous, soft cluckings, that it made my earlier attempts seem very inadequate indeed.

May

Sunday 3 May

It has been uncommonly cold, these last few days, though, thankfully, the rain seems to have exhausted itself. Tonight, it felt so welcome to eat our meal, sitting by the fire. It seemed slightly surreal, like being suspended between seasons, yet being in both Winter and Spring. My recent Birthday cards and gifts, still lay strewn about the room, and this all lent an air of some vaguely festive, or Christmassy atmosphere. Over the following days, I will occupy myself finding new homes in which to place my Birthday memories. I already have in mind the perfect setting for the exquisite gargoyle waterfall that Freddie and Marc have given me. And I think I shall transform it into something even more spectacular, by adding some purple or green coloured drops into the water. Then it will grace some shady, little corner of my recently revamped attic room.

Thursday 7 May

A land that is lonelier than ruin;
A sea that is stranger than death:

A. C. Swinburne

Today, together with some overseas friends, we decided on an outing to Dunwich. This disappearing village, so very loved by the poet A. C. Swinburne, greeted us with a grey and stormy sea. This same sea which so doggedly is advancing on Dunwich, and crumbling away its very existence.

Our friends, two Australians and one American, found the place intriguing, especially so, because two of them are writers themselves and so, their affinity with the memory of Swinburne was particularly strong.

This most favourite poet of mine, was irresistibly drawn to the sea. It always held a great fascination for him, throughout his life, and he wrote "By the North Sea" which I feel is a very close link between us. Despite the distance of the years since his death, on reading his poetry, I do not ever feel he has really left. His writing holds such vitality, richness and an ever present reality, for me, somehow. Prolific and endlessly rich, his verse flows effortlessly and generously. Reading Swinburne, we feel feasted by his words. As if he had prepared his poetic banquet just to lavish upon us, one finely-wrought image, one sinuously-sculpted rhythm, one ravishing, seductive, sense-shattering stanza upon another. Works like Faustine and Felise and Dolores can be read over and over, becoming richer and more powerful with each reading.

If you are not already familiar with Swinburne, I do hope you may feel drawn to discover him for yourself. I am certain he will enrich your life, as much as he has mine.

> *One ought, every day at least, to hear*
> *a little song, read a good poem, see a*
> *fine picture, and, if it were possible*
> *to speak a few reasonable words.*
>
> J. W. von Goethe

Friday 8 May

How much of life can go past just one small window. Today, Colin and I were in Freddie's office, when we heard the familiar call of the moorhen. She had climbed up from her ditch to visit the window that dispenses food, so magically. Freddie threw some bread for her, which she rapidly took down to her four very young chicks. Bald and fluffy, they can swim with amazing speed and grace. They looked comical, like little old men scurrying off to their secret nest, somewhere in all that mass of greenery and quiet water. Mother, of course, looked extremely proud and satisfied.

Tuesday 12 May

Though I was not at home on this date, I heard, on my return, of the heroic story that marked the day. Valiant Pharaoh fought off a fox!! Quite a feat I daresay. The act of protecting his precious harem cost him the loss of his regal tail feathers. All of them over nine inches in length, and of the most dazzling colours. Although I should not say this, he is my favourite cockerel; and now, he has gone up even more, in my estimation. Pharaoh the Beautiful. Pharaoh the Valiant. Pharaoh the Survivor.

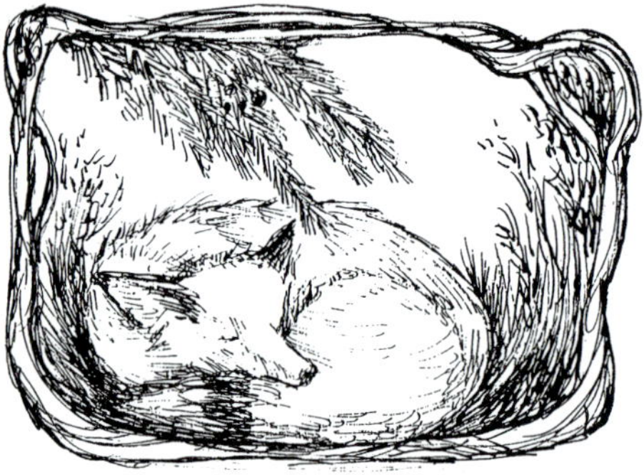

WEDNESDAY 13 MAY

Today, another very unusual event took place. And again, I missed it. It was seen and reported to me, by Colin. It seems that Jupiter must have been nosing where he shouldn't, and having got too close to a pheasant's nest, he was unlucky enough to disturb a very protective mother, who decided to attack back. Strange too, that Jupiter was intimidated enough to turn tail and run. She chased him away from the old orchard, past the house and barn and right through the young orchard. So she was very determined to get Jupiter as far as possible from her secret and tranquil nest. I only wish I had seen this hilarious spectacle.

THURSDAY 14 MAY

Driving home late this evening, a furry creature darted into the headlights. Its agile, young body, inexperienced and confused, did not know how to avoid us and kept running in front of our path, instead of veering away. In wondrous astonishment, we noted it was a baby fox. I was delighted by this rare sight. It must have been so afraid and anxious to find safety again. I was worried that it might stray too far from its familiar ground, so I suggested we turn off the lights for a moment while we stopped the car, to enable it to escape from us and from the light's glare. Sure enough, when we switched on again, it had disappeared. And I was so relieved to think it was probably more relieved than I, to find its comforting darkness, once again.

Friday 22 May

There is no such thing as an ordinary flower.

Charlotte Gray

Sharp sunlight. Bright colours. Blossoms that seem to rejoice. Vibrant greens that mist into smoky greys as distance subdues their searing energy into a hazy softness. All these, play tricks on the eyes. The senses. A magical world where everything seems to be happening at once. Joy and also a mellow restfulness. Glowing hues, yet also calming shades all about.

I stand still, in the middle of this emerald sea studded with buttercups. It seems the whole world has also come to a standstill. Jupiter is a little way further into the meadow. His raven-black coat, glossy and sparkling in the sunlight. He faces towards the sun, narrows his deep amber eyes, raises his head, and sniffs the air for something I shall never know. He is so intent. It appears to me as if the air is being drawn in and through all his body. Is he feeding on today's warm, airy elixir like some mythical creature from a non-corporeal world? For a long time, I enjoy just standing in that balmy breeze and watching the interconnectedness that so gracefully and perfectly enfolds us both.

June

THURSDAY 4 JUNE

How I love the surprise of a new find. Especially when it is some comical incident, perpetrated by one of our little tribe. Today, it was a once in a lifetime vision. A nearby bush shelters a small, meditating, stone Buddha. Calm and beautiful, he rests cross legged, surrounded by grass and wild flowers - some mystical-minded hen must have sensed his charisma, and felt drawn to lay her egg right by his lap. On seeing this, I was simply speechless. What strange consciousness led this hen to make her offering to the Serene One. To keep this thought with me, I took a photograph. Even as I shall look at it in years to come, I shall smile and wonder...

SUNDAY 14 JUNE

A perfect day, weather wise. And with two friends, I decide to explore beyond our usual boundaries. A picturesque drive and some cups of tea and coffee later, we arrive at Dedham, a village of spacious proportions and neat, elegant charm. The whole atmosphere is leisurely and carefree. I always like to absorb the mood of a new place by imagining myself living there; being part of its everyday movements and routine. One of the things I liked most, was the Parish Church. And in particular, its entrance door. For some reason it captivated me. So old and worn and smooth it was. Yet the carving was still exquisite in its subtly worn splendour.

Monday 22 June

Having enjoyed last week's explorations so much, I decided to see a little bit more of Suffolk, through Constable's eyes. Too many years have passed with my knowledge of him being only through his paintings. This seemed such a waste of an opportunity, when his birthplace was so close by. So today, we returned to the area that has been the sovereign of so many canvases, and spent more time delving inside the heart of those paintings. Walking through those same tree-shaded paths and by the same riverside that Constable made so famous. Walking past the place that once was his studio. Seeing Flatford Mill, once owned by his father, and now a centre for art students. Marvelling at how a humble working building dating from 1733 is now home to more budding artists.

But the highlight of my day has to be Lavenham, the town where Constable went to boarding school for a short time. A town of unimaginable beauty. Half-timbered Tudor houses and cottages take my breath away. They hardly seem real. Such variety and commanding presence; I feel as if I am looking at a film set. Though their angles and perspective is at times, crooked and strange, it is this same imperfection that somehow makes them so perfect. So dazed am I by this feast of bygone splendour that I cannot tear myself away from one street in order to go and look at the rest. By late afternoon I am still moving within this dream. The air is still and I am so filled with tranquillity, timelessness and a deep gratitude to know all this.

Monday 29 June

A friend has come to spend a few days and he just cannot get enough of all the "outdoors". Being restricted to London and the city routines, he finds this space and so much grass, trees and sky, a divine experience. He laughs all the time, and is constantly excited. He wants to go "for walks" all the time, and his eyes light up each time a pheasant, or an owl or a rabbit dart in and out of the landscape. For me, it is a joy to see his delight. And he picks up feathers to put in his cap and a fallen branch to make into a walking stick. He buys flowers from the roadside stalls and he admires the coppery gold of the sunsets and the dark of the Suffolk nights. I know he will return to his own life, shortly, but his spirit will remain strong and refreshed for a long time to come.

> *Let your mind alone,*
> *and see what happens.*
>
> Virgil Thomson

July

Saturday 11 July

Framlingham Castle and Medieval Archery go hand in hand. And today, I take an American friend to this "back in time" adventure. He is awed by his first visit to an English Castle and just cannot wait to try his hand at the ancient art of Archery. Then we climb the spiralling stone stairs to the very top and bask in the magnificence of the view, imagining how it must have felt to be a part of that distant life. When we can finally tear ourselves away from that vision, we descend, and crossing the courtyard, make our way out of the Castle gate and climb down towards the moat and the surrounding land. Inspired, uplifted and with so many memories to keep.

August

Tuesday 4 August

This summer has been far from hot and we had given up on seeing any baby swallows. But today Freddie told me that Maurice had noticed the swallows had begun to nest, as usual, high up in the Donkey Shed. Thankfully, the recent warmer weather must have made them optimistic and I take it also as a sign that maybe they can sense hotter days yet to come. I do not look forward to the prospect of heat, but I shall be listening out for those first, loud shrills coming from hungry little beaks.

Tuesday 11 August

Vigilant as ever, Maurice told me today that the red summer apples in the young orchard were ready for picking as the wasps were getting there first. So at about 6 o'clock this evening I went to see. I picked the first one and sank my teeth into it. It was so, so absolutely delicious. I understood why the wasps were so keen themselves. I just had not tasted such an apple for a very long time. I had to finish it right on the spot before I could continue picking any others. I took them in and left a very pretty one, complete with stalk and leaves attached, for Freddie to find when she comes in tomorrow morning.

SUNDAY 23 AUGUST

An incredibly blustery day but we still braved our way to Orford Castle. There was meant to be a Falconry Display but the elements proved too fierce to fly the birds and the event was cancelled. If the weather was unkind to humans, it must have been even more so for the waiting birds. Tied to their posts in hope of a break in the rain and wind, they tried to shelter by nodding their heads down, as their feathers were wildly ruffled in the gusting wind. I felt most sorry for the barn owl, who in his futile attempt to hide, tried to escape by tugging at the tie around his leg. Eventually the display had to be abandoned and we spent our time inside the castle, marvelling at the character of each chamber, hall, stairwell and most especially, the Chapel. It is always my most favourite destination. I like to sit quietly, awhile, and simply exist within its small and comforting space. So calming, so inviting. Its effect is never diminished. And I feel reassured and restored at the end of my time there. Once having left its safety we had to plunge anew into the driving rain. Running into the shelter of the Crown and Castle was our only relief. Here we warmed ourselves by drinking some hot chocolate before we could face the long drive back home. But all in all, it was a memorable day.

Thursday 27 August

A happy day!! For the Donkey Shed is a Nursery to the baby swallows once more. How well I love to see and hear them. The essence of Summer is so well captured in moments like this.

Later in the afternoon, Tracy called round. Her eyes gleaming as she said "I love coming here. Every time I come up your drive, things are different. New flowers to see, and shiny conkers and different colours that change all the time." And again I find myself enjoying comments like these, as they reaffirm the beauty and intelligence that is: Nature.

September

Friday 18 September

A staid and gallant dusk descends. Elegant and muted in its understated beauty. Jupiter is a little ahead of me and I look into the distance at the almost visible silence. A swift and ghostly form skims the tree tops. I focus well on it. It nears. It descends swiftly, flying closer towards me. It is the Barn Owl. I cannot believe its daring, as it heads straight in my direction. I stand still, to observe its flight. Never has such a bird come so close to me. It sends glorious shivers down my back. Tingling and feeling very privileged, I watch it swerve away and up into the tall trees again and finally out of sight.

Wednesday 23 September

I never quite saw fairy-folk
A-dancing in the glade,
Where, just beyond the hollow oak,
Their broad green rings are laid:

But, while behind that oak I hid,
One day I very nearly did!

Queenie Scott-Hopper

Sitting at my office desk, a flighty shimmer of something catches the corner of my eye. It is a tiny wren. I am surprised and happy to see this timid little bird alight so perkily into the chickens' drinking bowl. And my joy is prolonged, as I am treated to a bold dipping, splashing and bathing session. She skips up onto the stone rim and plunges into the water time and again, using the rocks inside as steps to land on before shaking her wet feathers and then diving in again. This confident display is uncharacteristic for this little beauty. She is merry and alone and obviously a very brave little creature. I wonder if this is to be a rare occasion or whether she will feel at ease enough to visit again.

Monday 28 September

Speaking with a friend in America today, I learnt that his brother's house in Alabama was hit by the hurricane that is sweeping that area. People are having to evacuate and temporarily live elsewhere. It all sounded so sad and I felt their distress keenly. Then, quite by chance, tonight I picked up a book to browse through before going to sleep. I was quite taken aback to find the very page I had opened at random, described the damage done by a hurricane, one Autumn. And how its victims dealt with and coped with their enforced, new way of life. Although the destruction affected many, the writer remarked on the positive aspects that the hurricane created. He noted how people then had to communicate directly with each other, because all lines of communication were down.

How they, for the first time, actually could hear the sound of trees moving, in the absence of traffic noise. And how the lack of city illumination enabled them to see the brilliant stars, embedded in a truly black sky. And so, while still dealing with the difficulties of an unwelcome situation, it does pay to look for and to accept the advantages or challenges that can result. We may not always be brave or strong enough for this, but at least we can try.

October

Thursday 1 October

The day was a very mild and pleasant one. And even if it had not been, I would still have felt happy because I had something to look forward to. At about half past midday I set off for Mill Common to meet with Mary, since we had long promised ourselves a leisurely lunch in Halesworth. When I arrived she was ready, but we spent some time catching up on the latest things that had changed in the house since my last visit. Also, taking a look at the beautiful splashes of colour which enliven her garden. After some time, we headed for Warners Wine Bar and as always when one enters, the inviting atmosphere immediately relaxed us further and then we had to face the delicious task of choosing from the fabulous menu for which Warners is famous. The afternoon progressed so happily in each other's company, and also from time to time, seeing or waving to someone whom we recognised. It is always so fine to see friendly faces, especially when it chances to be someone that we have not seen for a long time.

Wednesday 7 October

Above our heads, the soul of day
Moves softly through the autumn skies;
The earth gives up its green to grey,
And there before our stinging eyes,
It stirs and dies.

Kevin N. Roberts

Strange that it is only six days since my last journal entry, and yet the feel of the day is so different. There is a spacious sense of winter all around and as I went to see Freddie in her office, I saw my little wren once again, pirouetting on the rain gutter, looking in at us both, but no doubt feeling very secure on her side of the window glass.

The day has certainly progressed in blustery fashion. It is midnight and a very wild night it is too. It is just the right time to play some of my favourite music within my candle-lit attic, and the one I have chosen tonight is an astonishingly beautiful piece called 'Death in Venice', featuring the counter tenor Derek Lee Ragin. So powerful and overwhelming is the music, and the combined effect with the force of the elements outside creates a very rapturous and lofty sensation.

Friday 9 October

The end of another week comes and as the darkness of the late evening approaches, I remember the chickens and give them one last snack of lettuce and fruit cake. Amidst the usual clucking and fussing, they scurry around, tearing food out of each other's beaks, because somebody else's morsel of course always looks tastier than one's own. Then all of a sudden Poppy decides that it is bedtime and heads off at a fast pace towards the hen house. One or two of the others look quite startled, and breaking into a trot, decide to follow her. Very soon, there is a stampede as they all race each other, probably trying to avoid being last in order to find the most desirable position on the perch.

Tuesday 13 October

Finally all the pears are picked and Colin lays them out to store for the weeks to come. It is continually astonishing to me how abundant Nature is. She seems to produce all these marvellous fruits without any apparent effort. So naturally and almost miraculously. Never do you see a pear or an apple tree, struggling to fulfil its purpose, which must give a lot of credence to the quote that "You can tell that you are doing the right thing if it feels effortless."

I notice that there are not many days left before the clocks are changed, and that usually means that winter is truly on the way, so I think I had better make a note to check the fuel tanks tomorrow. I do not want to be in the anxious position in which I found myself last year, when just before Christmas I noticed that the oil in the Aga had almost all gone, and in a big panic I had to call up a friend who sorted out the problem for me and thanks to him I was able to have a rushed delivery. And so, happily, we were cosy at Christmas and also well fed.

Saturday 17 October

Received a warm and humorous letter from a friend in San Francisco today, together with some astonishing photographs of his garden, which he has so beautifully created from a mere heap of soil and rubble. He is so dedicated, or should I say obsessed, because as he himself says, he cannot leave it alone. And even when he is ill, he will go out and tend his precious blooms and vegetables. I had wonderful visions of him and his little dog scampering about in the rain and wind, muffled up with scarves and devotedly caring for his little plot, in that big city, on our shared planet.

Monday 26 October

I just wanted to remark on the forever welcome sight of a visiting peacock butterfly. As is their custom they contrive to surprise me with their brilliance and grace, each time I enter a room to find one angelically gliding, posing and coming to rest. Never can I take it for granted, and I always smile and feel so privileged to know they share my home.

November

SATURDAY 7 NOVEMBER

What better way to complete this journal than to go out with a bang, as the saying goes. I refer to the Bonfire and Fireworks Display that took place at our Westhall Village Green today. Although I did not attend, due to other obligations, I did manage to watch most of it from my attic. I cannot describe the exhilaration of the blending colours illuminating the sky, and the starbursts, and the giant snowflake shapes that lit up the surrounding countryside and blackened tree tops. Perhaps in retrospect it was better viewed from my window, for I managed to get an excellent overall effect, which would not have been so effective if I had been very close. It was magical and from time to time I could even hear some of the cheers from the crowd, although somewhat distantly. But this only lent the whole night an even more magnificent air of unison and joy.

Outside the garden
The wet skies harden;
The gates are barred on
The summer side:
Shut out the flower-time,
Sunbeam and shower-time;
Make way for our time,
The winter-tide.

Algernon Charles Swinburne

Companion Earlier Volume to "Pocketful Of Paradise"

At Home in Paradise **B105 £6.95**

At Home in Paradise is the irresistibly intimate journal of a sensitive and impassioned observer of Nature. From the attic of her 16th Century farmhouse in the English Countryside, Carmen records her impressions of the most subtle movements of Nature that ripple through her daily existence at the pace of some distant childhood summer, quietly yet profoundly influencing her Inner Life. Reminiscent of Thoreau's Walden in its appreciation of the Natural World as a nurturing, guiding and powerful force, Carmen's journal also calmly celebrates the beauty and sanctuary available in the 'tiny pleasures' of everyday life.

SpellBound **B104 £6.95**

Spellbound is a volume of magical, otherworldly beauty that will drench your soul with untamed yet holy insights into the shadowy, forbidden reaches of the human heart, revealing strange truths and extraordinary beauty. These poems, accented by lavish, inspiring artwork, are a wonderful introduction to the mystical revelations of Carmen's writings, viewing the world through the exquisitely melancholic haze of the lover's most rapturous dreams.

Luminarium

In Search of the DreamChild B101 £6.95

Through dreamlike images and the enchantment of language, one enters a mystical labyrinth, a kingdom that unveils the timeless power of light and innocence. Our inner journeys, our impassioned pleas, the sacredness of love and the sublime intensity of spiritual longings; are all movingly captured in over 50 poems. Profusely illustrated with Classic and Pre-Raphaelite images.

Gothic Dream B102 £6.95

Gothic Dream is an elegant and visionary glimpse of other realms. It is a bridge to a parallel dimension, a romantic world of inconsolable beauty and exquisite passions, wrapped in a web of lyrical sensuality. 120 pages of intriguing and enthralling poems, masterfully crafted and beautifully illustrated throughout with woodcuts and Pre-Raphaelite line drawings.

Sorrows of Fleeting Joy B103 £6.95

With the eloquence and depth of the great Romantic poets, Carmen unveils a singularly graceful insight into the human spirit's intensely passionate quest for immortal, loving union. Often erotic and sensuous, always poignant and captivating, these poems lure the reader into a sustained and compelling glimpse of a magical world where the souls of lovers ride the wings of Eternity in their desire to experience love on the level of the Divine. You will discover yourself within its inspired pages.

Quest For the Beloved **B106** **£6.95**

by Kevin N. Roberts

In this personal, philosophical approach to Carmen's Romantic and Metaphysical poetry, Professor Roberts takes an unprecedented look at the role of poetry as a tool for individual spiritual growth. The author reveals that, as a means of gaining a greater understanding of the human condition, the potential of Metaphysical poetry to unveil the nature of true romantic love, the loss of youthful innocence and the mysterious realm that awaits us all beyond death, is virtually without limit. At once authoritative, accessible and engaging, Quest for the Beloved will appeal not only to poetry lovers, but to anyone interested in following their bliss!